THE ART OF COMPING

DIE KUNST DES BEGLEITENS

L'ART DE L'ACCOMPAGNEMENT

JIM MCNEELY

THE ART OF COMPING

DIE KUNST DES BEGLEITENS

L'ART DE L'ACCOMPAGNEMENT

Workbook • Arbeitsbuch • Livret de travail

ADVANCE MUSIC

Cover Design: Traugott Bratic

Musical Notation: Walter Gruber

Published by Advance Music

D-7407 Rottenburg N., Germany

Production: Hans Gruber

Printed in West Germany

ISBN 3-89221-036-5

CONTENTS

INHALT

SOMMAIRE

Introduction

This book has been designed to fill a gap in jazz piano literature. It is a 'hands-on' workbook which enables you to practice and develop an often-neglected aspect of jazz piano playing: comping (i. e. accompanying as part of a jazz rhythm section). The Art Of Comping - Workbook has several aims. The first is to give you a chance to hear the author comp. Second, the text points out important aspects of the comping for each tune. Third, you get a chance to be involved in the comping process, by comping along with the same rhythm section, without the piano track. And finally, the book offers a number of specific suggestions for comping on each tune.

The six tunes here were recorded in the convential manner, with the piano well isolated from the other instruments. Since the recording is designed to demonstrate comping, there are no piano solos. In the mixing session, each tune was mixed in two ways. First, a normal mix was made. Then the tune was re-mixed with the piano track removed. What remains is a "three-person quartet", playing as if a pianist were comping. It`s up to you to supply the missing part!

The recording session was planned so as to keep the music spontaneous. We decided not to consciously try to comp in any particular way, or to force any rhythmic or harmonic elements into the music just for the sake of demonstration. We played naturally, the way we would on a gig. The result is 'the real thing'.

Rufus, Bobby, Art, Steve and Victor all do a great job here, and I thank them for that. Thanks also to Hans Gruber, for producing this session, and for making sure that Art made his plane on time!

Einleitung

Dieses Buch wurde geschrieben, um eine Lücke in der Jazzpiano-Literatur zu füllen. Es ist ein praxisorientiertes Arbeitsbuch, das Ihnen ermöglicht, einen oft vernachlässigten Aspekt des Jazzpianos zu üben und zu erweitern, nämlich das Begleiten [comping] eines Solisten. (Der Begriff 'Begleiten' bezieht sich in diesem Buch ausschließlich auf die Klavierbegleitung als Teil einer Jazz-Rhythmusgruppe).

Das Arbeitsbuch mit Tonträger "The Art of Comping" verfolgt mehrere Ziele: Erstens, können Sie dem Autor beim Begleiten zuhören. Zweitens, behandelt der Text wichtige Aspekte der Begleitung zu jedem Stück. Drittens, haben Sie die Möglichkeit selbst mit derselben Rhythmusgruppe zu spielen. Schließlich enthält das Buch spezifische Anregungen für das Begleiten jedes Stückes.

Die sechs Titel wurden auf die herkömmliche Art und Weise aufgenommen, dabei wurde das Piano gut isoliert. Da die Aufnahmen dazu da sind, die Begleitung zu demonstrieren, haben wir auf Klaviersoli verzichtet. Beim Abmischen wurde jedes Stück auf zwei Arten gemischt. Zuerst wurde eine normale Mischung hergestellt, anschließend eine zweite Mischung ohne Klavier. Was blieb, ist ein "Quartett mit drei Musikern", die so spielen, als ob ein Pianist begleiten würde. Sie können die fehlende Stimme ersetzen!

Um die Musik spontan zu halten, waren die Aufnahmen entsprechend vorausgeplant. Wir hatten uns entschlossen, nicht auf eine bestimmte Art und Weise zu begleiten, oder rhythmische und harmonische Elemente zum Zweck der Demonstration in die Musik hineinzuzwängen. Wir spielten natürlich, wie es bei einem Auftritt der Fall wäre. Das Resultat sind spontane, natürlich klingende Aufnahmen.

Rufus Reid, Bobby Watson, Art Farmer und Victor Lewis spielen großartig und ich danke ihnen dafür. Dank auch an Hans Gruber, der diese Aufnahmen produzierte und dafür sorgte, daß Art sein Flugzeug nicht verpaßte!

Introduction

Ce livret (à la fois recueil d'exercices et livret de travail) a été conçu pour combler une lacune dans la littérature pédagogique du "piano-jazz". Ce livret de travail constitue une veritable "force d'intervention" qui vous permettra de pratiquer et de développer un aspect très souvent négligé dans le jeu des pianistes de jazz: l'accompagnement (c'est-à-dire l'accompagnement en tant que partie d'une section rythmique de jazz).

"L'Art de l'Accompagnement" (en tant que livret de travail) a plusieurs objectifs. Le premier est de vous donner une chance d'entendre l'accompagnement de l'auteur. Deuxièmement, le texte met en évidence les importants aspects de l'accompagnement dans chacun des morceaux interprêtés. Troisièmement, vous avez la chance d'être engagé dans le processus de l'accompagnement, en accompagnant ces morceaux avec la même section rythmique, mais la piste du piano ayant été enlevée. Finalement, le livret offre un nombre important de suggestions spécifiques pour l'accompagnement de chaque morceau.

Les six morceaux, que l'ou trouve ici, furent enregistrés d'une manière conventionelle, avec le piano soigneusement isolé des autres instruments. Etant donné que l'enregistrement a été conçu pour montrer la manière dont ou doit accompagner, il n'y a pas de solo de piano. Pendant les séances de mixage, chaque morceau fut mixé de deux façons. En premier, on réalisa un mixage normal. Puis le morceau fut mixé à nouveau en enlevant la piste du piano. Ce qu'il reste un "vrai quartet à trois personnes" jouant comme si le pianiste était en train d'accompagner. A vous de fournir la partie manquante!

La séance d'enregistrement fut conduite de façon à garder à la musique un caractère spontané. Nous décidâmes de ne pas essayer consciemment d'accompagner d'une façon particulière, ou de mettre de force des éléments rythmiques ou harmoniques dans la musique juste pour des besoins de démonstration. Nous avons joué naturellement, de la manière dont on l'aurait fait en concert. Le resultat: "du vrai".

Rufus Reid, Bobby Watson, Art Farmer, Steve Erquiaga et Victor Lewis, ont tous fait un travail fantastique et je les remercie. Merci aussi à Hans Gruber de produire cette session et d'avoir veillé à ce que Art Farmer "attrape" son avion à temps!

General Suggestions

Each tune has specific suggestions and exercises to help you to put it to good use. But as a first step for any tune, listen to the recording *before* you look at the music. Become an *active* listener! Focus on the comping. Make observations and ask questions:

♦ The rhythmic placement of the comping: are the chords played on the beat, or off? Long durations, or short? Actively, or sparsely?

♦ Interaction of pianist with soloist: how much is there? How much imitation, call-and-response, punctuation of the soloist's phrases? How does the amount of interaction change from one soloist to another, or from one style of tune to another?

♦ How much space does the comping leave the soloist? Does this change over the course of a particular solo?

♦ Interaction of pianist with drums: how often do piano and drums hit the beginning of a section/chorus together? When they do, is it on '4-and' or directly on '1'? Is there imitation of figures? How do they play the turnarounds?

♦ Interaction with the bass: Do pianist and bassist play substitutions together? Does one play them without the other joining in? How does the bass register influence the comping?

♦ Voicings: do they change in terms of size, weight, energy, balance? How? When? Are there any special techniques used? Rolled chords, damper pedal, broken chords, chromatic inner voice movement? When? How do these techniques influence the effect of the comping, and of the overall sound of the quartet?

You may not notice all of these things; you may not have specific answers to the questions you raise. But at least you're starting to *listen with your head,* as well as to *think with your ears.*

Staying in the mode of the active listener, next play the piano-less version of the same tune. Does the music stand up without the rhythmic and harmonic input from the keyboard? Do these players really *need* a pianist to comp for them? I think not! Try imagine yourself playing piano with this group. What things would you do to enhance this music which already sounds so good without you? Now, go back to the 'piano' version of the tune. Does the comping enhance the music? What might you do differently than the pianist on the recording? Try not to think of harmonic ideas so much as rhythmic patterns and phrases. You might even comp rhythms on your legs, or a table top. Let your imagination flow! For each tune the chord symbols for both head

Allgemeine Empfehlungen

Zu jedem Stück gibt es spezifische Anregungen und Übungen, die Ihnen helfen sollen, sinnvoll damit zu arbeiten. Hören Sie sich aber zu jedem Stück zuerst die Aufnahme an, *bevor* Sie die Noten ansehen. Werden Sie ein *aktiver* Hörer! Konzentrieren Sie sich auf die Klavierbegleitung. Beobachten Sie und stellen Sie sich Fragen:

♦ Die rhythmische Plazierung der Begleitung: Werden die Akkorde auf dem Schlag, davor oder danach gespielt? Lange oder kurze Notenwerte? Wird viel oder eher sparsam gespielt?

♦ Interaktion des Pianisten mit dem Solisten: Wieviel Interaktion gibt es? Wieviel Imitation, Frage-Antwort, Interpunktion der Phrasen des Solisten? Wie ändert sich die Stärke der Interaktion von einem Solisten zum anderen oder von einem Stil eines Stückes zu einem anderen?

♦ Wieviel Freiraum läßt die Begleitung dem Solisten? Ändert sich das im Verlauf eines bestimmten Solos?

♦ Interaktion des Pianisten mit dem Schlagzeug: Wie oft kommen Klavier und Schlagzeug zusammen am Anfang eines neuen Teils oder Chorus an? Falls ja, ist es auf '4und' oder direkt auf dem ersten Schlag? Gibt es Imitation rhythmischer Figuren? Wie spielen Sie die Turnarounds?

♦ Interaktion mit dem Baß: Spielen der Pianist und der Baßist Substitutionen gemeinsam? Spielt sie einer von beiden, ohne den anderen? Wie wirkt sich die Lage, in der der Baß gerade spielt, auf die Klavierbegleitung aus?

♦ Voicings: Ändern Sie sich in Bezug auf die Anzahl der Töne, Gewichtung, Energie, Balance? Wie? Wann? Werden spezielle musikalische Techniken verwendet? Arpeggierte Akkorde, Dämpfpedal, chromatische Bewegung der inneren Stimmen? Wann? Wie verändern diese Techniken die Wirkung der Begleitung und den Gesamtcharakter des Quartetts?

Möglicherweise werden Ihnen diese Dinge nicht alle auffallen. Vielleicht haben Sie auch keine spezifischen Antworten auf Ihre Fragen, aber wenigstens fangen Sie an mit Ihrem *Verstand zu hören* und mit Ihren *Ohren zu denken.*

Bleiben Sie vorläufig in der Rolle des Zuhörers und hören Sie sich als nächstes die Version desselben Stückes ohne Klavier an. Kann die Musik ohne den harmonisch-rhythmischen Beitrag des Pianos bestehen? *Brauchen* diese Musiker tatsächlich einen Pianisten, der sie begleitet? Ich glaube nicht!

Suggestions générales

Chaque morceau possède ses propres suggestions et exercices spécifiques pour vous aider à en faire un bon emploi. Mais comme premier pas pour n'importe quel morceau, écoutez l'enregistrement *avant* de regarder la musique. Devenez un auditeur *actif.* Dirigez toute votre attention sur l'accompagnement. Faites des observations et posez des questions:

♦ Le placement rythmique de l'accompagnement: les accords sont ils placés sur le temps, ou après le temps? Leur durée est longue ou courte? Le placement se fait-il d'une façon active ou clairsemée?

♦ L'interaction du pianiste avec le soliste: comment est-il présent? Y-a-t-il beaucoup d'imitations, de questions et réponses, de ponctuations des phrases du soliste? L'importance des interactions change-t-elle d'un soliste à un autre ou d'un style de morceau à un autre?

♦ Combien d'espace l'accompagnement donne-t-il au soliste? Est ce que cela change au cours d'un solo particulier?

♦ L'interaction du pianiste avec la batterie: combien de fois le piano et la batterie touchent le début d'une section ou d'une structure ensemble? Quand ils le font est-ce sur la partie faible du 4ème temps ou directement sur le premier temps? Y-a-t-il imitation dans les motifs rythmiques? Comment jouent-ils les "turnarounds*"?

♦ Interaction avec la basse: Est-ce-que le piano et la basse jouent les substitutions d'accords ensemble? Est-ce-que l'un joue ces substitutions et l'autre pas? Dans quelle mesure le registre de la basse influence-t-il l'accompagnement?

♦ Harmonisations des accords: ces harmonisations changent-elle en termes de dimensions, de poids, d'énergie, d'équilibre? Comment? Quand? Emploie-t-on pour cela des techniques particulières? Roulement d'accords, pédales d'expression, accords éclatés, mouvement chromatique d'une voix intérieure? Quand s'en sert-on? Comment ces techniques affectent-elles l'accompagnement, et le son d'ensemble du quartet?

Vous pouvez remarquer toutes ces choses; et vous pouvez ne pas avoir de réponses spécifiques aux questions que vous posez. Mais ou moins vous commencez *d'écouter avec votre tête,* et *de penser avec vos oreilles.*

Tout en restant un auditeur actif, joue ensuite le même morceau avec la version où le

*Ce sont les deux dernières mesures d'une section ayant un mouvement harmonique cyclique.

and solo form are written over a double staff. This is done in case you want to write out chord voicings for the comping. Some of the symbols might be unfamiliar to you; or, you might be trying out new voicings. But try to get away from reading written voicings as soon as possible. It's more effective to play simple voicings with spontaneity than it is to read more complicated ones. Besides, using simple, familiar voicings leaves you more of your concentration for tuning in to the soloist, Rufus, and Victor. Another suggestion: using a tape machine, make a tape of yourself comping with the piano-less tracks. Listen to the result with a critical, honest ear. How does the comping help the group? What could be improved? Put your ego to rest, listen honestly, and you're bound to hear some ways to improve your comping!

Finally, it should be noted here that, although a workbook like this might help you improve your comping, there is really no substitute for playing with real people, in jam sessions or gigs. Real people never play a song the same way twice. To comp with real people you need the ability to react and suggest *spontaneously* to what you are hearing, while it's all being made up on the spot. This can only be done in the pressure cooker of live performance.

Stellen Sie sich vor, Sie würden mit dieser Gruppe mitspielen. Was würden Sie tun, um die Musik zu verbessern, die ohne Sie schon gut klingt?

Hören Sie sich nun noch einmal die Version mit Klavier an. Verbessert die Klavierbegleitung die Musik? Was würden Sie anders als der Pianist der Aufnahme spielen? Versuchen Sie nicht so sehr an harmonische Ideen zu denken, vielmehr an rhythmische Motive und Phrasen. Sie können sogar auf Ihren Schenkeln oder auf der Tischplatte Rhythmen spielen. Lassen Sie Ihrer Vorstellungskraft freien Lauf.

Bei jedem Stück sind die Akkordsymbole für den Melodie- und den Soloteil über dem leeren Klaviersystem notiert - falls Sie selbst Akkord-Voicings notieren wollen. Einige Symbole sind vielleicht neu für Sie, oder Sie möchten neue Voicings ausprobieren. Versuchen Sie jedoch, sobald wie möglich von den notierten Voicings wegzukommen. Es ist effektiver, spontan einfache Voicings zu spielen als komplizierte abzulesen. Zudem lassen Ihnen einfachere Voicings mehr Konzentration für den Solisten und für Rufus Reid und Victor Lewis.

Ein anderer Vorschlag: Nehmen Sie sich beim Begleiten der pianolosen Aufnahmen mit einen Tonbandgerät auf. Hören Sie sich das Ergebnis kritisch, ehrlich und mit offenen Ohren an. Wie hilft die Begleitung der Gruppe? Was könnte verbessert werden? Stellen Sie Ihr Ego ab, hören Sie ehrlich zu und Sie werden einiges hören, wie Sie Ihre Begleitung verbessern können!

Zum Schluß sollte noch erwähnt werden, daß Ihnen ein Arbeitsbuch wie dieses helfen wird, Ihr Begleiten zu verbessern. Es gibt jedoch keinen Ersatz für das Spielen mit einer Gruppe, bei Sessions oder bei Auftritten. MUSIKER spielen ein Stück kein zweitesmal gleich. Um 'wirkliche' Musiker zu begleiten, benötigen Sie die Fähigkeit, in dem Moment in dem alles entsteht, zu reagieren und *spontan* zu antworten auf das, was Sie hören. Das kann nur unter dem enormen Druck eines Auftrittes passieren.

piano est supprimé. Est-ce que la musique reste valable, tient encore sa place sans l'apport harmonique et rythmique du clavier? Ces musiciens ont-ils *réellement besoin* d'un pianiste pour faire l'accompagnement derrière eux? Je ne le pense pas! Essayez de vous imaginer jouant du piano avec ce groupe. Que feriez vous pour mettre en valeur cette musique qui sonne si belle sans vous?

Maintenant, retounez à la version du morceau comportant le piano. Est-ce que l'accompagnement réhausse la musique? Que feriez vous différement du pianiste de l'enregistrement? Ne pensez pas trop en termes d'idées harmoniques mais plutôt en termes de phrases et motifs rythmiques. Vous pouvez même jouer de la batterie sur vos cuisses, ou sur le dessus de la table. Laissez couler votre imagination!

Sur chaque morceau les symboles des accords pour le thème et les solos sont écrits sur une portée double. Ceci afin que vous puissiez écrire, si vous le désirez, leurs harmonisations. Certains de ces symboles vous seront peut-être peu familiers, voire inconnus; ou vous essaierez avec eux de nouvelles harmonisations, de nouveaux renversements. Mais essayez de vous écarter, le plus vite possible, de la lecture des harmonisations écrites. Il est beaucoup plus efficace de jouer des accords simples avec spontanéité que de lire des harmonisations plus complexes. De plus, jouer des harmonisations simples qui vous sont familières, vous permettra de vous concentrer davantage, pour vous mettre en accord, en phase, avec le soliste, Rufus Reid, et Victor Lewis.

Une autre suggestion: employez un magnétophone, enregistrez vous accompagnant la version sans piano? Ecoutez le résultat avec une oreille critique et honnête. Comment l'accompagnement aide le groupe? Que puis-je améliorer? Mettez votre moi, votre égo au repos, écoutez honnêtement, et vous serez obligé d'entendre certaines façons d'améliorer votre accompagnement!

Finalement, on devra remarquer à ce moment là que: bien que ce manuel de travail puisse m'aider à améliorer ma façon d'accompagner, il n'existe pas quelque chose qui puisse se substituer, remplacer au le fait de jouer avec des musiciens vivants, dans des jam-sessions ou des représentations. Les musiciens en chair et en os ne jouent jamais une mélodie, un thème deux fois de la même façon. Pour accompagner des musicien, qui jouent réllement vous devez posséder la capacité de réagir *spontanément* à ce que vous entendez et de suggérer vos propres idées, pendant que tout se crée sur le champ. Ceci ne peut se faire que sous la pression très forte qui s'exerce sur vous lorsque vous jouez en public.

A Note About The "Suggested Voicings"

The voicings in the "Suggested Exercises" sections of the book appear as whole-notes. A solid black note (Ex. 1) indicates an individual note which may be *added* to the voicing. An individual whole-note, or group of whole-notes, in brackets (Ex. 2) indicates a note or a group which may be played *instead* of a note or group of notes in the original voicing.

Ein Hinweis zu den "Voicing Empfehlungen"

Die Voicings in den Bereichen "Voicing-Empfehlungen" sind in ganzen Noten notiert. Eine ausgefüllte Note (Bsp. 1) kann dem Voicing *hinzugefügt* werden. Eine einzelne ganze Note, oder eine Gruppe von ganzen Noten in Klammern (Bsp. 2) kann/können *anstelle* einer Note oder einer Gruppe von Noten des ursprünglichen Voicings gespielt werden.

Un remarque sur les "harmonisations suggérées"

Les harmonisations dans "les exercices suggérés" de ce manuel sont écrites sous forme de rondes. La notre "noircie" entre parenthèses (Ex.1) indique que cette note peut être *ajoutée* à l'harmonisation. Une note individuelle ayant la valeur d'une ronde, ou un groupe de rondes, entre parenthèses (Ex. 2) indiquent une note ou un groupe de notes pouvant être joués à la place d'une note ou d'un groupe de notes dans l'harmonisations originale.

Example 1 **Beispiel 1** **Exemple 1**

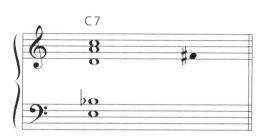 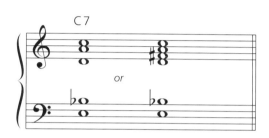

Example 2 **Beispiel 2** **Exemple 2**

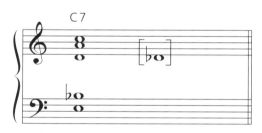 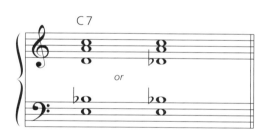

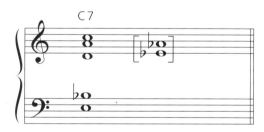 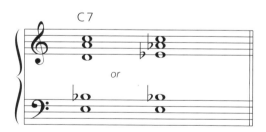

9

Jim McNeely

BLUES FOR WANDA

Art Farmer, Soloist

About The Tune:

This is a twelve-bar blues in B♭. The head has a specific harmonic progression: note the V7-IV7 in bars 9 and 10, and the ♭VII7 -VII7 turnaround in the last two measures. These changes are used for the first two choruses of each solo, followed by 'normal' blues changes for the rest of the solo. Solo order is Art Farmer, five choruses, Rufus Reid, three, then four choruses of trading fours with Victor Lewis.

About The Comping:

♦ The comping on the head either reinforces accents in the melody, or fills holes.

♦ There is a lot of off-beat rhythmic placement in the comping.

♦ Note the figure at the end of Art's solo chorus IV:

The piano starts it, drums pick it up towards the end, and we hit the beginning of the next chorus together. Octave voicings in the piano give more impact (see "Suggested Exercises" D–6).

♦ Note the way that the comping continues *into* the bass solo. This helps provide continuity through the transition.

♦ The dominant pedal F is suggested at the ends of choruses III and V of Art's solo, as well as chorus III of Rufus' solo. This provides tension throughout the turnaround, and helps the feeling of movement into the next chorus.

♦ Note the change in dymanics and register in comping for the bass solo. In general, the comping is softer, and in a higher register..

♦ Common substitutes are used: relative II–7, tritone, E°7 leading into F–7 (see "Suggested Exercises" E).

♦ The rythmic duration of the voicings is mostly short. Occasionel long values occur.

♦ Note the comping coming of the bass solo: the dominant pedal (F), increase in volume, and use of the damper pedal all help to build into the next section.

Über das Stück:

"Blues For Wanda" ist ein 12taktiger Blues in B♭. Der Melodieteil hat eine spezielle harmonische Progression. Beachten Sie die V7-IV7 Verbindung in den Takten 9 und 10 und den ♭VII7-VII7 Turnaround in den letzten beiden Takten. Diese Progression wird für die ersten zwei Chorusse jedes Solos verwendet, danach folgt die 'normale' Bluesprogression für den Rest des Solos. Die Reihenfolge der Soli: Art Farmer - fünf Chorusse, Rufus Reid - drei, gefolgt von vier Chorussen im viertaktigen Wechsel mit Victor Lewis.

Über die Begleitung:

♦ Die Begleitung während des Melodieteils hebt entweder Akzente der Melodie hervor oder füllt Pausen.

♦ Es gibt sehr viel rhythmische Deplazierung in der Begleitung.

♦ Achten Sie auf die Figur am Ende von Arts viertem Chorus:

Das Klavier fängt damit an, das Schlagzeug nimmt sie gegen Ende auf und wir landen gemeinsam am Anfang des nächsten Chorus. Oktav-Voicings erzielen mehr Wucht (siehe "Empfohlene Übungen" D-6).

♦ Beachten Sie, wie die Begleitung in das Baßsolo *hinein* fortgesetzt wird. Das sorgt für Kontinuität während des Übergangs.

♦ Der Dominantorgelpunkt F wird am Ende des dritten und vierten Chorus' von Arts Solo und im dritten Chorus von Rufus' Solo angedeutet. Das sorgt für Spannung während des Turnarounds und trägt dazu bei, daß ein Gefühl der Bewegung in den nächsten Chorus hinein entsteht.

♦ Achten Sie auf den Dynamik- und Registerwechsel der Begleitung für das Baßsolo. Im allgemeinen wird sie leiser und befindet sich in einer höheren Lage.

♦ Gebräuchliche Akkordsubstitute werden verwendet. Kleinterz- (II–7) und Tritonusverwandtschaft: E°7 leitet zu F–7 über (siehe

A propos du morceau:

C'est un blues de 12 mesures en Si♭ (B♭). Le thème possède une progression d'accords spécifique: remarquez de la 'descente' d'accords V7-IV7 dans les mesures 9 et 10, et le cycle d'accords ♭VII7-VII7 dans le "turnaround" des deux dernières mesures. Ces Changements d'accords sont utilisées dans les deux premières structures de chaque solo, suivis par des structures de blues avec un changement d'accord "normal" pour le reste du solo. L'ordre des solos est le suivant: Art Farmer 5 structures, Rufus Reid, 3 structures, puis 4 structures d'échanges de 4 mesures (4/4) avec Victor Lewis.

A propos de l'accompagnement:

♦ L'accompagnement sur le thème renforce les accents de la mélodie, ou remplit les espaces de silence ('les trous').

♦ Il y a un grand nombre de figures rythmiques de l'accompagnement placées après le temps.

♦ Remarquez la figure rythmique à la fin de la structure IV du solo de Art:

Le piano commence ce rythme, la batterie "l'attrape au vol" vers la fin et nous marquons ensemble le début de la structure suivante. L'harmonisation en octaves au piano donne un impact plus grand (voir "Exercices suggérés" D-6).

♦ Remarquez la façon dont l'accompagnement continue *à l'intérieur* du solo de basse. Ceci aide à fournir une continuité pendant la transition.

♦ La pédale de dominante (fa) est suggérée à la fin des structures III et V du solo de Art Farmer, ainsi que dans la structure III du solo de Rufus Reid. Ceci fournit une tension pendant le "turnaround", et aide à la sensation de mouvement dans la structure suivante.

♦ Remarquez les changements de nuances et de registre dans l'accompagnement pour le solo de basse. En général, l'accompagnement est plus doux et dans une tessiture plus aignë.

♦ Des substitutions d'accords bien connues sont

- In trading fours with Victor: sometimes the comping starts on the 'and' of 4, sometimes on the downbeat. Sometimes the phrase ends on the 'and' of 4, sometimes on the downbeat of the next bar.

- The voicing of the final chord of the coda has the root in the bottom. Since it isn't moving to another chord, this is a good way to 'anchor' the chord, and give it a sense of finality.

- "Empfohlene Übungen" E).

- Rhythmisch sind die Voicings hauptsächlich kurz, nur gelegentlich kommen längere Notenwerte vor.

- Beachten Sie die Begleitung aus dem Baßsolo heraus. Der Dominantorgelpunkt F, eine zunehmende Lautstärke und die Verwendung des Dämpfpedals tragen zum Aufbau in den nächsten Chorus hinein bei.

- Beim viertaktigen Phrasenaustausch mit Victor Lewis beginnt die Klavierbegleitung manchmal auf '4und', manchmal auf '1', manchmal endet die Phrase auf '4und' und manchmal auf der '1' des nächsten Taktes.

- Das Voicing des Schlußakkordes der Coda hat den Grundton ganz unten. Da nach diesem Akkord kein weiterer mehr kommt, ist es gut, den Akkord zu 'verankern' und ihm so einen Schlußcharakter zu geben.

- employées, le relatif mineur II–7, la substitution du triton, accord de E°7 aboutissant à F–7 (voir "Exercices suggérés" E).

- La durée rythmique des harmonisations est la plupart du temps courte. Des accords de longue durée sont employés occasionellement.

- Remarquez l'accompagnement qui se dégage à la fin du solo de basse: La pédale de dominante (Fa), l'augmentation du volume sonore, l'emploi de la pédale étouffoir, tout cela aide à augmenter l'intensité, de l'accompagnement à l'intérieur de la nouvelle section.

- Les échanges de 4/4 avec Victor montrent que parfois l'accompagnement "démarre" après le quatrième temps (sur la partie faible du temps) et parfois sur le premier temps. Parfois la phrase musicale se termine sur la fin du 4ème temps et parfois sur le premier temps de la mesure suivante.

- L'harmonisation de l'accord final de la coda montre la tonique à la basse de l'accord. Etant donné qu'il ne se déplace pas vers un autre accord c'est un moyen efficace "d'ancrer" l'accord et de lui donner un caractère définitif.

BLUES FOR WANDA
Format

Head (2x's)

‖: B♭ Blues

Trumpet Solo (2x's)

:‖: B♭ Blues (Head Changes)

(3x's)

:‖: B♭ Blues (Normal) :‖

Bass Solo (2x's)

‖: B♭ Blues (Head Changes)

:‖ B♭ Blues (Normal)

Trading 4th's with Drums (4x's)

‖: B♭ Blues (Normal) :‖

D.C. al Coda

BLUES FOR WANDA

Jim McNeely

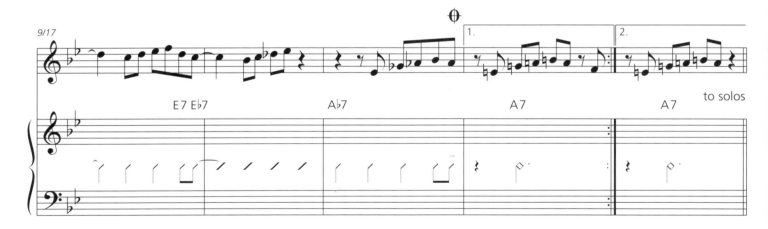

Solos:

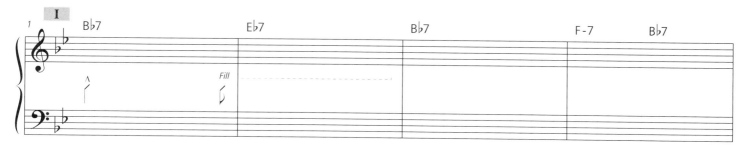

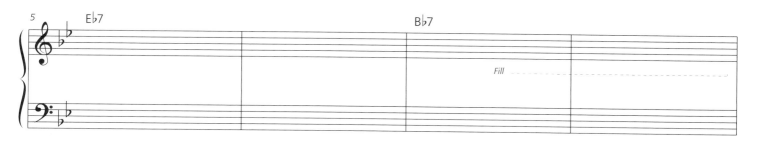

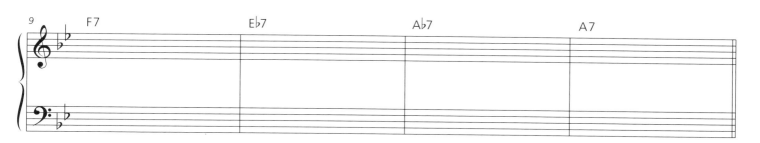

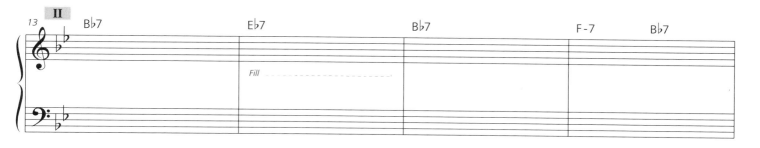

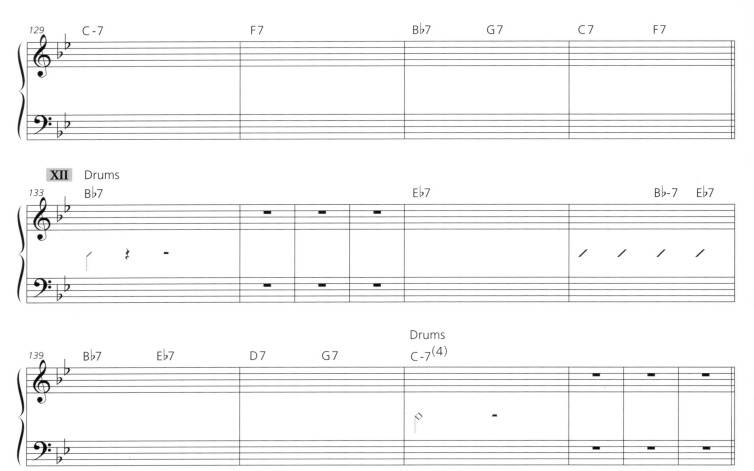

D.S. al Coda

Suggested Exercises:

A. Try some different rhythmic treatments of your chord voicings.

    1. Exactly *on* the beat:

    2. Constantly anticipated on the 'and' of the previous beat:

    3. Mixed placement.

    4. All long duration:

    5. All short duration:

    6. Constantly on '2and' and '4and':

Hear how playing in each of these ways produces a different rhythmic feel in the music.

B. If you find it difficult to comp through all the written chord symbols, simplify the progression to

Empfohlene Übungen:

A. Probieren Sie unterschiedliche rhythmische Anwendungen Ihrer Akkord-Voicings aus.

    1. Exakt *auf* dem Schlag:

    2. Ständig antizipiert auf der 'und' des vorherigen Schlages:

    3. Gemischte Plazierung.

    4. Nur längere Notenwerte:

    5. Nur kürzere Notenwerte:

    6. Ständig auf '2und' und auf '4und':

Hören Sie darauf, wie dadurch jedesmal ein anderer rhythmischer Charakter der Musik entsteht.

B. Sollte es Ihnen schwer fallen, alle Akkord-symbole zu spielen, vereinfachen Sie die Progression:

Exercices suggérés:

A. Essayezdes traitements rythmiques différents de l'harmonisation de vos accords.

    1. Exactement *sur* le temps:

    2. Constamment anticipés sur la partie faible du temps précédent:

    3. Placement mixte des accords (sur le temps et anticipés).

    4. Tous les accords sont de longue durée:

    5. Tous les accords sont de courte durée:

    6. Les accords sont placés constamment sur la partie faible du 2ème et 4ème temps:

Ecoutez comment chacune de ces façons de jouer donne un caractère rythmique différent à la musique.

B. Si vouz trouvez difficile d'accompagner en vous servant de tous les changements d'accords écrits, simplifiez la progression de la façon suivante.

After you can play these, add G-7 to m. 8, and C–7 - F7 to m. 12. Then, try adding E♭7 in m. 2, and F–7 - B♭7 in m.4. Slowly, you can work your way into the written progression.

Nachdem Sie das spielen können, nehmen Sie in Takt 8 G–7 und in Takt 12 C–7 - F7 dazu. Versuchen Sie als nächstes in Takt 2 E♭7 und in Takt 4 F–7, B♭7. So können Sie sich langsam an die notierte Progression heran-arbeiten.

Quand vous saurez jouer ceci, ajoutez Sol-7 (G–7) à la mesure 8, et Do–7 - Fa7 à la mesure 12. Puis, essayez d'ajouter Mi♭7 à la mesure 2 et Fa–7 - B♭7 dans la mesure 4. Lentement, vous pourrez trouver la façon de jouer une progression écrite.

C. Try preceding each chord with a voicing a half-step above:

C. Versuchen Sie vor jedem Akkord ein Voicing zu spielen, das einen Halbtonschritt höher liegt.

C. Essayez de faire précéder chaque accord avec un autre accord situé un demi-ton au dessus:

D. Try different sizes of voicings. Some suggestions for each of the most common chords in this progression:

D. Probieren Sie unterschiedliche Voicing-Grössen aus. Hier sind einige Anregungen für die gebräuchlichsten Akkorde dieser Progression:

D. Essayez des accords de tailles différentes. Voici quelques suggestions pour les accords les plus employés dans cette progression:

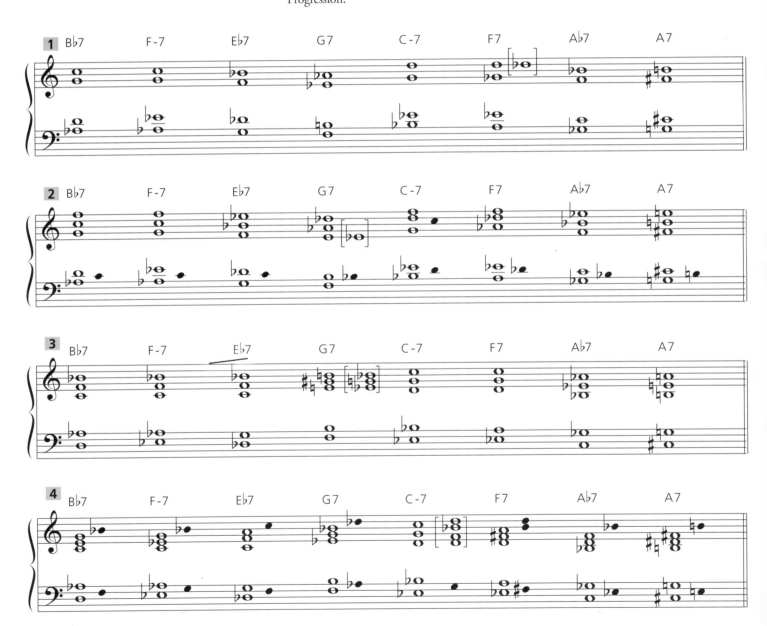

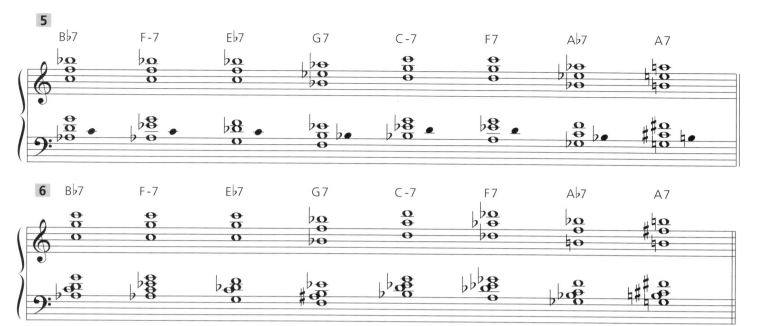

5 Bb7　　F-7　　Eb7　　G7　　C-7　　F7　　Ab7　　A7

6 Bb7　　F-7　　Eb7　　G7　　C-7　　F7　　Ab7　　A7

7. As you become more familiar with each set of voicings, try shifting to a larger size in each successive chorus (start the shift in the turnaround a bar or two before the new chorus begins). Hear how the increase in size helps the energy of the group to build.

E. Try different substitutions. Listen for the effect they have on the tune. Some suggestions:

  1. Measure 2, F–7

    Measure 4, B–7, E7

    Measure 7, D7$^{\sharp 9}$

    Measure 9, C$^{\sharp}$–7, F$^{\sharp}$7

7. Wenn Sie mit einer Gruppe von Voicings vertrauter sind, versuchen Sie nach jedem Chorus zu größeren Voicings zu wechseln. Beginnen Sie damit beim Turnaround, ein oder zwei Takte vor dem nächsten Chorus. Hören Sie darauf, wie der Wechsel der Voicing-Größe dazu beiträgt, die Energie der Gruppe zu steigern.

E. Experimentieren Sie mit verschiedenen Stellvertreterakkorden. Hören Sie darauf, welche Wirkung das auf die Musik hat:

  1. Takt 2, F–7

    Takt 4, B–7, E7

    Takt 7, D7$^{\sharp 9}$

    Takt 9, C$^{\sharp}$–7, F$^{\sharp}$7

7. Comme vous devenez plus familier avec chaque série d'harmonisations, essayez de changer pour une taille d'accords plus grande à chaque nouvelle structure (commencez le changement dans la mesure ou les deux mesures avant le commencement d'une nouvelle structure. (Cette mesure ou ces deux mesures s'appellent un "turnaround" dans la musique de jazz; il est formé avec une progression d'accords qui ramène en "tournant" vers le premier accord. Ecoutez comment l'augmentation en taille des accords aide à augmenter la puissance du groupe.

E. Essayez différentes substitutions d'accords. Ecoutez l'effet qu'elles produisent sur le morceau. Quelques suggestions:

  1. Mesure 2, F–7

    Mesure 4, B–7, E7

    Mesure 7, D7$^{\sharp 9}$

    Mesure 9, C$^{\sharp}$–7, F$^{\sharp}$7

2.

| Bb7 | A7 | Bb7 | B-7 E7 | Eb7 | Eø A7 | D7$^{\sharp 9}$ | Ab7 G7 | C#-7 F#7 | C-7 F7 | Ab7 G7 | Gb7 F7 |

3. All 7sus4 chords:

| Bb7sus | ℅ | ℅ | ℅ Eb7sus | ℅ | Bb7sus | G7sus | Gb7sus | F7sus | Bb7sus | Bb7sus B7sus |

4.

| BbΔ | Aø D7 | G-7 (C7) | F-7 Bb7 | Eb7 | ℅ | D-7 | G7 | C#-7 F#7 | F#-7 B7 | Bb7 Db7 | GbΔ B7 |

F. Try different amounts of rhythmic activity:

1. Comp sparsely through the first chorus (one voicing every two bars). Make the next chorus a little less sparse (one per bar). The next chorus a little busier (two per bar). The next even busier (three per bar).

2. Now, reverse the process: very busy, less busy, even less, sparse

3. Comp very sparsely through the entire tune.

4. Comp very busily through the entire tune.

Hear how the level of sparseness/business in your comping effects the overall rhythmic feeling and shape of the tune.

G. The more you comp through the tune, try to catch some of the more audible details played by the other members of the group:

1. Art Farmer leaves some nice holes in his lines, especially in the first three choruses. A chord or two in the right spot (marked 'fill') works well here.

2. Chorus IV, mm. 1-4, Rufus' bass line. Try:

F. Experimentieren Sie mit unterschiedlichen rhythmischen Aktivitäten:

1. Begleiten Sie im ersten Chorus sparsam (ein Voicing in jedem zweiten Takt). Im nächsten Chorus etwas weniger sparsam (ein Voicing pro Takt). Im nächsten Chorus etwas geschäftiger (zwei Voicings pro Takt). Und im nächsten Chorus noch geschäftiger (drei Voicings pro Takt).

2. Kehren Sie nun diesen Prozess um: sehr geschäftig - weniger geschäftig - noch weniger geschäftig - sparsam.

3. Begleiten Sie während des ganzen Stückes sehr sparsam.

4. Begleiten Sie während des ganzen Stückes sehr geschäftig.

Hören Sie darauf, wie sich der Grad der Sparsamkeit/Geschäftigkeit Ihrer Begleitung auf den rhythmischen Gesamtcharakter und auf den Verlauf des Stückes auswirkt.

G. Nachdem Sie mehrmals mit der Aufnahme begleitet haben, sollten Sie versuchen einige leichter hörbare Details der anderen Musiker zu erfassen.

1. Art Farmer läßt in seinem Solo einige 'nette' Pausen, besonders in den ersten drei Chorussen. Ein oder zwei Akkorde an der richtigen Stelle (in den Noten als 'fill' gekennzeichnet), passen gut.

2. Chorus IV, Takte 1-4, Rufus Reids Baß Linie. Probieren Sie:

F. Essayez des niveaux d'activité rythmique différents:

1. Accompagnez d'une façon très espacée la première structure (un accord toutes les deux mesures). La deuxième structure sera un peu plus remplie (un accord par mesure). La structure suivante sera plus animée (deux accord par mesure). La structure suivante encore plus active (trois accords par mesure).

2. Maintenant, inversez le processus: très actif, moins actif, encore moins actif, clairsemé.

3. Accompagnez d'une façon très clairsemée tout au long du morceau.

4. Accompagnez d'une façon très active tout au long du morceau.

Ecoutez comment le degré d'activité ou d'inactivité dans votre accompagnement affecte l'ensemble du caractère rythmique et la forme du morceau.

G. Le plus vous accompagnez le morceau, et le plus vous devez essayer d'entendtre les détails les plus audibles joués par les autres membres du groupe:

1. Art Farmer laisse de jolis espaces dans ses lignes improvisées, particulèrement dans les trois premières structures. Un accord ou deux au bon endroit (marqué "fill"; fill signifie remplir; avec de la musique bien sûr!) cela fonctionne très bien, ici.

2. Structure IV, mesures 1-4, ligne de basse de Rufus Reid. Essayez:

|Bb7 Bo7 |C-7 C#o7 |D-7 EbΔ |Eo7 / F-7 Bb7 |

or / oder / ou

|Bb7 B7 |C7 C#7 |D7 Eb7 |E7 F7 |

3. Art reaches his peak with a high Bb in chorus V, m. 1.

Help him get there by building the turnaround just before that spot.

4. Chorus V, mm. 1-2, Rufus again.

Try:

3. Art erreicht seinen Höhepunkt im ersten Takt des fünften Chorus mit einem hohen Bb. Helfen Sie im, indem Sie im Turnaround, gerade vor dieser Stelle, steigern.

4. Chorus V, Takte 1-2, wiederum Rufus Reid. Versuchen Sie:

3. Art Farmer atteint son point culminant avec un contre-Sib aigu dans la structure V, mesure 1. Aidez le à l'atteindre en "construisant" le "turnaround" qui se place juste avant ce point, c'est à dire en ajoutant votre propre énergie à celle du soliste.

4. Structure V, mesure 1-2, pour Rufus Reid encore. Essayez:

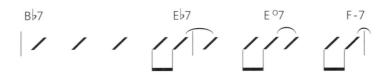

5. comp with Victor at the turnarounds in choruses IV (mm. 11-12) and V (mm. 11-12).

6. Art ends his solo with the phrase:

5. Begleiten Sie bei den Turnarounds im vierten und fünften Chorus zusammen mit Victor Lewis (jeweils Takte 11-12).

6. Art Farmer beendet sein Solo mit dieser Phrase:

5. Accompagnez Victor Lewis pendant les "turnarounds" dans les structure IV (mesures 11-12) et V (mesures11-12).

6. Art Farmer termine son solo avec la phrase:

How might you harmonize this?
Try:

Wie würden Sie das harmonisieren?
Probieren Sie:

Comment pouvez-vous harminiser cela?
Essayez:

7. Chorus VIII, mm. 11-12. Rufus is ending his solo, leading the group into the fours with Victor. Help him here by building the volume, increasing the size of the voicings, and using a dominant pedal.

8. Choruses IX-XII: When trading with the drums, try to comp on the downbeat after Victor ends his four bars. Don't wait for him and Rufus to show you the downbeat. For an added challenge, try comping through Victor's four-bar solos.

7. Chorus VIII, Takte 11-12. Rufus beendet sein Solo und führt die Gruppe in den viertaktigen Phrasenaustausch mit Victor. Helfen Sie ihm dabei, indem Sie die Lautstärke steigern, das 'Gewicht' der Voicings vergrößern und einen Dominant-orgelpunkt spielen.

8. Chorusse IX-XII: Versuchen Sie beim Phrasenaustausch mit dem Schlagzeug nach Victor Lewis' Solo auf der '1' zu spielen. Warten Sie nicht darauf, daß er und Rufus Reid Ihnen die '1' zeigen. Als zusätzliche Herausforderung können Sie während Victor Lewis' viertaktigen Soli begleiten.

7. Structure VIII, mesures 11-12. Rufus Reid est en train de finir son solo, conduisant le groupe à des échanges de quatre mesures avec Victor Lewis. Aidez le en augmentant le volume, en vous servant d'accords plus fournis et en employant une pédale de dominante.

8. Structures IX-XII: Pendant les échanges de quatre mesures avec la batterie, essayez de placer un accord sur le temps après que Victor ait terminé ses quatre mesures. N'attendez pas après Victor Lewis et Rufus Reid pour vous montrer le premier temps. Pour un défi encore plus important, essayez d' accompagnier pendant les quatre mesures de solo.

Blues For Wanda

Robert Watson

CROSSROADS

Robert Watson, Soloist

About The Tune:

This is a twenty measure, medium tempo swinger. Although the tune's harmony doesn't move in any radical way, it contains a couple of surprise moves that keep you on your toes. Solo order is Robert Watson, three choruses, and Rufus Reid, two.

About The Comping:

- There are specific rhythmic figures in the head: mm. 1-8, and also mm. 13-20. These figures are generally not used in the solos.

- The voicings tend to grow in size as the alto solo builds, then get smaller at the end of the solo, to help the transition into the bass solo.

- Rhythmically the comping gets more active as the alto solo goes on, peaking in the third chorus.

- There is little, if any, substitution in the harmony. Substitution is more likely to be used in a 'standard', which 1. functions as a common point of reference for the players and listeners, and 2. contains recognizable, functional progressions.

- Occasionea broken figures between the two hands help energize the rhythmic aspect of the comping.

- Though not indicated in the original piano part, it seemed appropriate to play a fill in measure 11.

- The energy is sustained into the bass solo. Small voicings are used for the bass.

- In the second out-chorus, measure 9, the chord and cymbal crash happened spontaneously - a lucky accident!

Über das Stück:

"Crossroads" ist ein 20taktiger *medium Tempo Swing*. Obwohl sich die Harmonik des Stückes nicht drastisch bewegt, enthält sie einige Überaschungen, die Sie auf Zack halten werden. Die Reihenfolge der Soli: Robert Watson, drei Chorusse und Rufus Reid zwei.

Über die Begleitung:

- Der Melodieteil enthält in den Takten 1-8 und 13-20 spezielle rhythmische Figuren. Diese Figuren werden während der Soli in der Regel nicht verwendet.

- Die Voicings werden gewichtiger, sobald sich das Altsolo steigert und nehmen gegen Ende des Solos wieder ab, um beim Übergang zum Baßsolo mitzuhelfen.

- Mit der Fortdauer des Altsolos wird die Begleitung rhythmisch aktiver und erreicht ihren Höhepunkt im dritten Chorus.

- Es gibt, falls überhaupt, wenig harmonische Substitution. Sie wird eher bei Standards verwendet, die erstens eine Referenzfunktion für Musiker und Hörer erfüllen, und zweitens auf bekannten funktionalen Akkordfolgen aufgebaut sind.

- Gelegentlich verleihen gebrochene Figuren, aufgeteilt auf beide Hände, dem rhythmischen Aspekt der Begleitung Energie.

- Obwohl es in der ursprünglichen Klavierstimme nicht verzeichnet war, schien es passend, in Takt 11 ein *fill* zu spielen.

- Die Energie wird bis in das Baßsolo hinein beibehalten, für das kleinere Voicings verwendet werden.

- Beim zweiten Restatement der Melodie ereignete sich in Takt 9 spontan ein 'Zusammenstoß' zwischen einem Akkord und einem Beckenschlag - ein glücklicher Unfall!

A propos du morceau:

C'est un morceau de vingt mesures au tempo médium et swingué. Bien que l'harmonie du morceau ne fasse pas de mouvements d'une façon qui soit radicale, il contient quelques mouvements surprise qui vous obligent à la vigilance. L'ordre des solos est le suivant: Robert Watson, trois structures et Rufus Reid deux.

A propos de l'accompagnement:

- Il y a quelques figures rythmiques spécifiques dans le morceau, mesures 1-8 et aussi mesures 13-20. Ces figures rythmiques ne sont généralement pas employées pendant les solos.

- Les harmonisations ont tendance à augmenter en taille en même temps que le solo de "sax alto" se construit; à la fin du solo l'intensité du solo diminue pour aider à la transition avec le solo de basse.

- Rhythmiquement, l'accompagnement devient plus actif à mesure que le solo d'alto se développe pour atteindre son point culminant dans la troisième structure.

- Il y a très peu, voir pas, de substitutions dans l'harmonie. La substitution d'accords et plutot employée dans un morceau "classique" ("standard" de jazz) qui: 1. fonctionne comme un point de référence commun pour les musiciens et les auditeurs. 2. et contient des progressions d'accords fonctionelles et reconnaissables.

- Des figures de rythmes brisés occasionelles entre les deux mains aident à donner de l'energie à l'aspect rythmique de l'accompagnement.

- Bien qu'il ne soit pas indiqué dans la partie de piano originelle il semble adéquat de jouer un motif de remplissage dans la mesure 11.

- L'énergie est maintenue pendant le solo de basse. Des accords à la texture plus petite sont employés pour le solo de basse.

- Dans la seconde structure de fin à la mesure 9, l'accord et le coup de cymbale accéntué se produisent en même temps, spontanément, un heureux accident!

CROSSROADS
Format

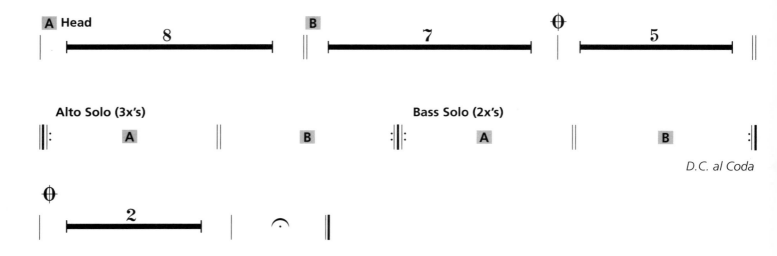

A Head

| 8 |

B

| 7 |

⊕

| 5 |

Alto Solo (3x's)

| **A** | **B** |

Bass Solo (2x's)

| **A** | **B** |

D.C. al Coda

⊕

| 2 | 𝄐 |

CROSSROADS

Robert Watson

2nd time to solos

Solos:

A

1 C7sus　　FΔ　　　　E7♭9　　A13　　　　B♭Δ　　E♭Δ　　E-7　　A7sus

5 C7sus　　FΔ　　　　E7♭9　　A13　　　　B♭Δ　　E♭Δ　　A-7　　A♭-7

B

9 G-7　　D-7　　　　Bø　　E7　　　　A-7　　　　B♭Δ

13 A-7　　A♭-7　　G-7　　C7sus　　E7♭9　　　　FΔ

17 E7♭9　　　　　　FΔ　　　　　　A7sus　　　　D-7　　G7sus

after solos D.C. al Coda

Suggested Exercises:

A. Try using upper chromatic neighbors to the voicings in places such as mm. 1, 2, 5, 6, 9, 11, 12, 15, 16, 17, and 18.

A few examples:

Empfohlene Übungen:

A. Probieren Sie die oberen chromatischen Nachbar-Voicings an folgenden Stellen: Takt 1, 2, 5, 6, 9, 11, 12, 15, 16, 17 und 18.

Ein paar Beispiele:

Exercices suggérés:

A. Essayez d'employer des accords chromatiquement et situés au dessus des accords placés dans les mesures telles que 1, 2, 5, 6, 9, 11, 12, 15, 16, 17 et 18.

Quelques exemples:

B. Use half-step approaches to each chord. This can be quite a challenge with this progression. (See Blues For Wanda "Suggested Exercises" C).

C. Certain voicings may be embellished with diatonic movement, especially those in measures 1, 3, 5, 7, 11, 12, 16, and 18. For example:

B. Nähern Sie sich jedem Akkord über einen Halbtonschritt. Bei dieser Akkordfolge kann das eine ganz schöne Herausforderung sein (siehe Blues For Wanda "Empfohlene Übungen" C).

C. Bestimmte Voicings können mittels diatonischer Bewegung umspielt werden, ganz besonders die in den Takten 1, 3, 5, 7, 11, 12, 16 und 18, z.B.:

B. Employez des approches par demi-ton pour chaque accord. Ceci sera à coup sûr un défi avec une telle progression. (Se reporter à Blues for Wanda, "exercices suggérés" C).

C. Certains accords peuvent être embellis par un mouvement diatonique; particulièrement ceux des mesures 1, 3, 5, 7, 11, 12, 16 et 18. Par exemple:

D. Try some moving internal chromatic lines in mm. 2, 3, 6, 7, 8, 9, 10, 11, 12, 13, and 15. For example:

D. Probieren Sie in den Takten 2, 3, 6, 7, 8, 9, 10, 11, 12, 13 und 15 chromatische Bewegung der inliegenden Stimmen aus, z.B.:

D. Essayez des lignes mélodiques chromatiques ayant un mouvement interne dans les mesures 2, 3, 6, 7, 8, 9, 10, 11, 12, 13 et 15. Par exemple:

E. In measures 15 and 17 the ascending minor-third technique works for diminished scale voicings:

E. In den Takten 15 und 17 passen aufsteigende Mollterzen zu Voicings der verminderten Skala:

E. Dans les mesures 15 et 17, la technique d' harmonisation en tierces mineures ascendantes fonctionne pour les harmonisations réalisées avec la gamme diminuée.

F. Try comping using an ostinato rhythm through the whole chorus. Some examples:

F. Versuchen Sie einen ganzen Chorus mit einem Ostinatorhythmus zu begleiten. Einige Beispiele:

F. Essayez d'accompagner en employant un rythme obstinato pendant toute la durée du solo. Quelques exemples:

Or, try these rhythms, based on groups of three eighth-notes:

Oder probieren Sie diese Rhythmen. Sie sind in Gruppen mit je drei Achtel unterteilt:

Ou essayez ces rythmes, basés sur des groupes de trois croches:

G. Try using one of these ostinati (F) for the first eight bars of the chorus. Then at measure 9 move into more active, varied rhythms and larger voicings. This is an effective way to establish tension-and-release.

H. Keep the energy sustained *into* the bass solo. *You* form the bridge that links the alto and bass solos together.

I. In the coda, for a final chord you might try one of these chords, as they work with the saxophone's melody notes:

G. Experimentieren Sie mit einem der Ostinati (F) in den ersten acht Takten des Chorus. Gehen Sie dann in Takt 9 zu abwechslungs-reicheren, aktiveren und größeren Voicings über. Das ist ein effektiver Weg, um Spannung auf- bzw. abzubauen.

H. Behalten Sie die Energie bis in das Baßsolo *hinein* bei. *Sie* bauen die Brücke, die das Alt-mit dem Baßsolo verbindet.

I. In der Coda können Sie für den Schluß-akkord einen der folgenden Akkorde probieren - sie passen zu den Melodietönen des Saxophones:

G. Essayez d'employer un de ces obstinati (F) pour les huit premièrs mesures de la structure. Puis à la mesure 9, dirigez vous vers des rythmes variés et plus actifs et aussi vers des accords plus larges. Ceci est un moyen efficace pour établir tension et détente.

H. Maintenez l'énergie *pendant* le solo de basse. *Vous* êtes le pont qui relie le solo d'alto et de basse.

I. Dans la coda, pour l'accord final, vous pouvez essayer un de ces accords, étant donné qu'ils conviennent aux notes mélodiques du saxophone:

J. Some sample voicings for this tune: J. Einige Voicing-Beispiele für dieses Stück: J. Quelques exemples d'accords pour ce morceau.

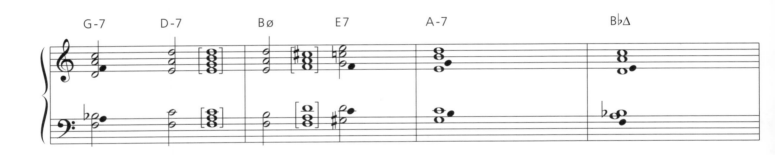

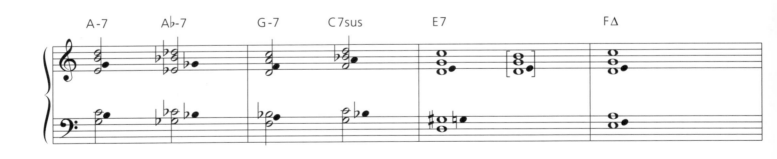

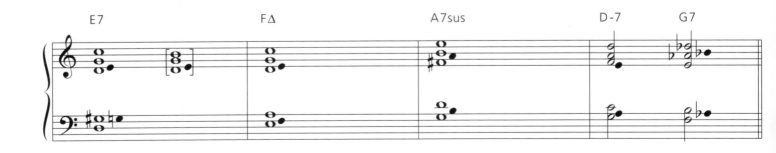

Octave voicings:

Oktav-Voicings:

Octave structures:

*Although these notes "clash" with the given chord, they are okay in the high register of the right hand.

*Obgleich sich diese Töne mit dem gegebenen Akkord eigentlich nicht vertragen, können sie in der hohen Lage mit der rechten Hand gespielt werden .

*Bien que ces notes produisent une dissonance extrême avec l'accord donné, elles sont acceptables dans le registre aigu de la main droite.

Thelonious Monk/Cootie Williams
'ROUND MIDNIGHT
Art Farmer, Soloist

About the tune:

This arrangement of Thelonious Monk's classic, courtesy of Art Farmer, represents a 'typical' version of the tune: the first six bars of the introduction are standard, and appear on a number of Monk's own recordings of the tune. Bars G and H come from the famous Miles Davis arrangement (from "Round About Midnight", Columbia). The ending is also standard, although Art's decending bass line two bars before the end is different than the cycle of II–7 - V7's that most people play.

The changes in the tune itself are pretty standard. Monk himself changed certain elements of the harmony over the years, so it's difficult to say what the 'real' changes are. What we have here, however, is what most experienced jazz musicians play. Note especially the last two bars of the bridge (mm. 23-24), in which we use Monk's original changes, not Miles' well-known cycle (Bb–7, Eb7, Ab–7, Db7 / F♯–7, B7, Fø, Bb7).

Solo order is: Art Farmer - one chorus, Rufus Reid - half chorus.

About The Comping:

♦ The underlying feel of this performance is a slow, evenly divided 4/4. The comping features lots of long, sustained sounds.

♦ For the flugelhorn solo, the rhythm section shifts to a double-time feel. The comping changes here, becoming more 'rhythmic' and syncopated. It also uses shorter, more detached figures to support the overall sense of motion in the double-time feel.

♦ The size of the voicings generally increases during the last ten measures of Art's solo, coming down at the end in order to help pave the way into the bass solo.

♦ There are many instances of internal chromatic movement, especially in the head chorus. See mm. 7, 11, 17, 24, 26, and 27, as well as m. 23 of the out chorus. The slow feel and tempo of the head gives the ear more time to hear and 'digest' these moving lines.

♦ The slow tempo enables the comping to cover a wide range of the keyboard. This gives the comping a greater melodic sense, as well as an

Über das Stück:

Das Arrangement dieses Thelonious Monk 'Klassikers' stammt von Art Farmer. Es repräsentiert eine 'typische' Version dieses Stückes. Die ersten sechs Takte der Einleitung sind standardisiert und in einigenen von Monks eigenen Aufnahmen zu hören. Die Takte G und H stammen vom berühmten Miles Davis Arrangement ("Round About Midnight", Columbia). Der Schluß ist ebenfalls allgemein gebräuchlich, obgleich Arts absteigende Baßlinie, zwei Takte vor dem Schluß, anders ist als der Zyklus von II–7 - V7 Verbindungen, den die meisten Musiker spielen.

Die Akkordfolge des Stückes selbst ist weitgehend standardisiert. Monk selbst hat im Laufe der Jahre bestimmte Elemente der Harmonien geändert, deshalb ist es schwierig zu sagen, welche die 'richtige' Akkordfolge ist. Wie dem auch sei, was wir hier haben, ist das, was die meisten erfahrenen Jazzmusiker spielen. Achten Sie ganz besonders auf die letzten zwei Takte des Mittelteils (Takte 23-24), in denen wir Monks ursprüngliche Akkordfolge verwenden und nicht Miles' bekannten Zyklus (Bb–7, Eb7, Ab–7, Db7 / F♯–7, B7, Fø, Bb7).

Die Reihenfolge der Soli: Art Farmer - ein Chorus, Rufus Reid - ein halber Chorus.

Über die Begleitung:

♦ Dieser Aufnahme liegen gleichmäßig unterteilte, langsame 4/4 zugrunde. Die Begleitung enthält viele, lang gehaltene Klänge.

♦ Für das Flügelhorn-Solo wechselt die Rhythmusgruppe zu einem *double-time feel*. Die Begleitung ändert sich dabei und wird 'rhythmischer' und synkopierter. Zudem werden kürzere, detachierte Figuren verwendet, um den Gesamteindruck der Bewegung im *double-time feel* zu unterstützen.

♦ Die Voicings werden in den letzten 10 Takten von Arts Solo gewichtiger und nehmen dann wieder ab, um den Weg in das Baßsolo zu bahnen.

♦ Es gibt viele Fälle mit chromatischer Bewegung der inliegenden Stimmen, ganz besonders im Melodieteil (siehe Takt 7, 11,

A propos du morceau:

Cet arrangement de ce classique de Thelonious Monk, courtoisie de Art Farmer, représente une version "typique" de ce morceau: Les six premières mesures de l'introduction sont "standard", habituelles et apparaissent dans de nombreuses versions enregistrées par Thelonious Monk. Les mesures G et H proviennent du fameux arrangement de Miles Davis (de l'album "Round About Midnight", Columbia). La fin est aussi "standard", bien que la fin soit différénte du cycle de II–7 - V que la plupart des musiciens joue.

La progression d'accords dans le morceau lui-même est plutôt standard. Monk lui-même changea certains éléments de l'harmonie au cours des années, et il est difficile de dire quel est le "réel" changement d'accords. Ce que nous avons ici, cependant, est ce que les musiciens les plus experimentés, jouent. Remarquez particulièrement les deux dernières mesuresdu pont (section B, mesures 23-24), dans lesquelles nous utilisons le changement d'accords origínel de Monk et non le très connu cycle de Miles Davis. (Bb–7, Eb7, Ab–7, Db7 / F♯–7, B7, Fø, Bb7).

L'ordre des solos est: Art Farmer une structure, Rufus Reid, la moitié d'une structure.

A propos de l'accompagnement:

♦ Le caractère sous-jacent que l'on trouve tout au long de l'exécution de ce morceau est celui d'un morceau lent, à 4 temps et dont les croches sont jouées d'une façon égale; (binaire). L'accompagnement met en evidence un grand nombre de sons longuement soutenus.

♦ Dans le solo de flugelhorn (bugle), la section rythmique change pour un tempo donnant l'impression d'un tempo doublé. l'accompagnement change ici, devenant plus "rythmique" et syncopé. Il emploie aussi des figures rythmiques plus courtes plus détachées pour aider à conserver le sens général de mouvement dans le tempo à caractère doublé.

♦ La dimension des harmonisations augmente généralement dans les dix dernières mesures du solo de Art Farmer, diminuant à la fin du

expanded sense of textural variety.

- Occasional upper register 'splashes' add color to the comping (e. g. mm. 8, 18, and 23).

- Note the places where the comping fills holes in the flugelhorn solo, especially mm. 3, 4, 7, 8, 9, and 18. Also, note the interaction between piano and flugelhorn in mm. 25-27.

- Comping for the bass solo consists of two lines for the first two measures. The reat of the solo is accompanied by a legato 'curtain' of sound*, with occasional moving chromatic lines.

- A notable spontaneous moment occurs in the 'out' bridge. In m. 18, Rufus starts a figure derived from the introduction, and the piano picks it up in the second half of the bar. In m. 20, Rufus starts it up again. This time the piano lets him finish it, then answers with chromatic motion into the A♭-7 of the next measure.

17, 24, 26 und 27 sowie Takt 23 des letzten Melodieteils). Der langsame Charakter und das Tempo des Melodieteils lassen dem Gehör mehr Zeit, diese Bewegungen zu hören und zu 'verdauen'.

- Das langsame Tempo ermöglicht zudem, einen größeren Bereich der Tastatur zu verwenden. Was wiederum der Begleitung einen melodischeren Charakter und eine erweiterte Struktur verleiht.

- Gelegentliche 'Farbtupfer' im hohen Register kolorieren die Begleitung zusätzlich (z.B. Takt. 8, 18, und 23).

- Achten Sie auf Stellen, wo die Begleitung Pausen des Flügelhorn-Solos füllt, ganz besonders in den Takten 3, 4, 7, 8, 9 und 18. Beachten Sie auch die Interaktion zwischen Piano und Flügelhorn in den Takten 25 bis 27.

- Die Begleitung des Baßsolos besteht in den ersten zwei Takten aus zwei Linien. Der Rest des Solos wird mit einem *legato-curtain-sound**, mit gelegentlichen Linien begleitet, die sich chromatisch bewegen.

- Ein erwähnenswerter, spontaner Moment ereignete sich im Mittelteil des letzten Melodieteils. In Takt 18 beginnt Rufus Reid eine Figur, die von der Einleitung stammt. Das Piano nimmt sie auf und in der zweiten Hälfte von Takt 20 fängt Rufus wieder damit an. Das Piano läßt sie ihn diesesmal zuende führen und antwortet mit einer chromatischen Bewegung in den Akkord A♭-7 des nächsten Taktes hinein.

solo de façon à préparer le chemin pour le solo de basse.

- Il y a de nombreuses manifestations de mouvements chromatiques internes, particulièrement dans la structure d'exposition du thème. Observez les mesures 7, 11, 17, 24, 26 ainsi que la mesure 23 le la structure finale. Le cractère lent du tempo dans l'exposition du thème donne à l'oreille plus de temps pour entendre et "digérer", absorber, ces lignes mouvantes.

- Le tempo lent permet à l'accompagnement de couvrir une large tessiture sur le clavier. Ceci donne à l'accompagnement un sens mélodique plus grand, ainsi qu'un sens étendu de la variété des textures.

- Des "éclaboussures" ocassionelles dans les registres aigus du piano ajoutent de la couleur à l'accompagnement. (voir mesures 8, 18, et 23).

- Remarquez les endroits ou l'accompagnemet remplit les espaces laissés par le solo de flugelhorn mesures 3, 4, 7, 8, 9 et 18. Remarquez aussi l'interaction entre le piano et le flugelhorn dans les mesures 25-27.

- L'accompagnement pour le solo de basse est formé de deux lignes pendant les deux premières mesures. Le reste du solo est accompagné par un "rideau de son" avec des lignes occasionelles qui se déplacent chromatiquement.

- Un moment de spontanéité remarquable se produit sur le pont de la structure finale. Dans la mesure 18, Rufus Reid commence une figure tirée de l'introduction et le piano l'attrape au passage dans la seconde moitié de la mesure. Dans la mesure 20, Rufus Reid recommence. Cette fois le piano le laisse terminer, puis répond avec un mouvement chromatique sur le La♭-7 de la mesure suivante.

---

*Marc Johnson's term

*Marc Johnson's Begriff [curtain = Vorhang]

'ROUND MIDNIGHT
Format

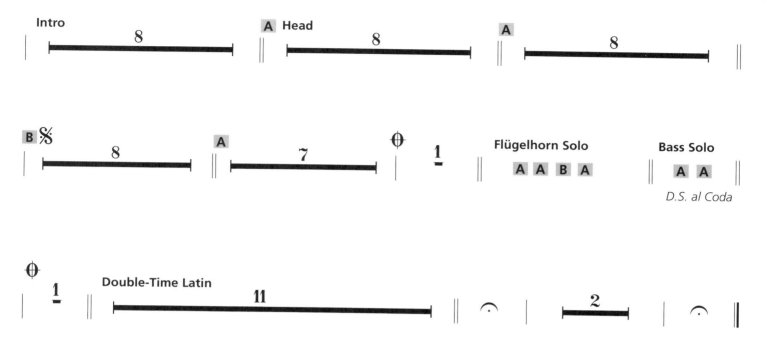

* On the recording, the piano plays the first chord before the flügelhorn enters. When playing with the piano-less recording, listen for the first two beats of the melody, as if they were pick-ups, playing the chord on the third beat of measure A.

* Bei der Aufnahme spielt das Piano den ersten Akkord bevor das Flügelhorn einsetzt. Wenn Sie mit der pianolosen Version spielen, hören Sie auf die ersten beiden Schläge der Melodie - so als ob es ein Auftakt wäre - und spielen den Akkord auf dem dritten Schlag von Takt A.

* Sur l'enregistrement, le piano joue le premier accord avant que la trompette n'entre. Quand vous jouez avec l'enregistrement sans piano, écoutez les deux premiers temps de la mélodie comme s'ils étaient une levée, et jouer sur le troisième temps de la mesure A.

'ROUND MIDNIGHT

Thelonious Monk / Cootie Williams

Solos:

I (Flügelhorn)

1
| Eb- | Eb-/D | Eb-/Db | Cø | Ab-7 | Db7 | Cø | F7 | B-7 | E7 | Bb-7 | Eb7 |

5
| Ab-7 | Db7 | GbΔ | G7#9 | Ab9 | Cø | F7 | Bb7b5 |

9
| Eb- | Eb-/D | Eb-/Db | Cø | Ab-7 | Db7 | Cø | F7 | B-7 | E7 | Bb-7 | Eb7 |

13
| Ab-7 | Db7 | GbΔ | G7#9 | Ab9 | Cø | F7 | Bb7b9 4 - 3 | EbΔ |

17
| Cø | F7 | Bb7b5 | Cø | F7 | Bb7b5 |

21
| Ab- | Ab-/Gb | Fø | Bb7 | Cø | F7 | Db7(9) | B7(9) | Ab-7 | Db7 | Fø | Bb7 |

D.S. al Coda

Suggested Exercises:

A. Try comping *without* using the damper pedal at all. You'll surprise yourself at how much you can connect voicings together using only your hands!

B. Really *listen* to Art's solo, and try to achieve a feeling of dialogue with him. Listen especially for the holes in his phrases, as well as any long notes in his lines.

C. When Art's solo starts, play only long, sustained chords for a chorus. How does this affect the feel of the music? Now comp through his solo again, this time using short, more syncopated figures. Feel the difference?

D. Keep comping *through* the end of Art's solo to provide a connection into Rufus' solo.

E. A ballad gives a pianist a chance to explore chromatic linear motion inside the voicings. Here are a few examples:

Empfohlene Übungen:

A. Versuchen Sie ganz *ohne* Dämpfpedal zu begleiten. Sie werden erstaunt sein, wie oft Sie Voicings miteinander verbinden können, indem Sie nur Ihre Hände benützen!

B. *Hören* Sie konzentriert auf Art Farmers Solo und versuchen Sie eine Art Dialog mit ihm aufzubauen. Hören Sie ganz besonders auf Pausen und auf lange Töne in seinen Phrasen.

C. Spielen Sie im ersten Chorus von Art Farmers Solo nur lange, ausgehaltene Akkorde. Welche Wirkung hat das auf den Charakter der Musik? Spielen Sie nun kürzere, synkopierte Figuren. Spüren Sie den Unterschied?

D. Begleiten Sie *weiter* bis zum Ende von Arts Solo, um einen Übergang in Rufus Reids Solo hinein zu schaffen.

E. Eine Ballade gibt dem Pianisten die Möglichkeit, innere, lineare chromatische Bewegung zu erkunden. Hier ein paar Beispiele:

Exercices suggérés:

A. Essayez d'accompagner en ne vous *servant* pas de la pédale étouffoir. Vous serez surpris vous-même de voir combien il et possible de relier les accords entre eux uniquement en se servant des mains.

B. *Ecoutez* réellement le solo d'Art Farmer, et essayez de parvenir à un sentiment de dialogue avec lui. Soyez particulièrement attentif aux espaces de silence laissés dans ses phrases, ainsi qu'à toutes les longues notes contenues dans ses lignes mélodiques.

C. Quand le solo d'Art Farmer commence, jouez seulement des accords longs et soutenus pendant une structure. Comment cela affecte-t-il le caractère de la musique? Maintenant accompagnez son solo, en employant cette fois des figures rythmiques courtes et plus syncopées. Ressentez vous la différence?

D. Continuez à jouer *pendant* la fin du solo de Art Farmer pour fournir une liaison au solo de Rufus Reid.

E. La ballade donne à un pianiste la chance d'explorer des mouvements linéaires chromatiques à l'intérieur des harmonisations d'accords. En voici quelques exemples:

F. You might try adding these passing chords in measure 21,

F. Sie können die folgenden Durchgangs-akkorde in den Takten 21

F. Vous pouvez essayer d'ajouter ces accords de passage dans la mesure 21,

Ab-7   Gb-7   Fø   Bb7   B°7

and in measure 23.

und 23 hinzufügen.

et dans la mesure 23.

Db7   C7   B7   A-7

G. Approaching chords from a half-step above is a very common practice in ballad playing. Here are some typical places to apply this technique:

1. Intro, mm. C and E:

G. Einen Akkord über einen Halbtonschritt von oben anzuspielen, ist bei Balladen sehr gebräuchlich. Hier sind einige typische Stellen, wo diese Technik angewendet werden kann:

1. Einleitung, Takte C und E:

G. Employer des accords d'approche situés un demi-ton au dessus est une pratique très courante dans l'interprétation des ballades. Voici quelques endroits particuliers pour appliquer cette technique:

1. Introduction, mesures C et E:

Abø   Gø   C7   Gbø   Fø

2. Measure 3:

2. Takt 3:

2. Mesures 3:

Cø   Gb7   F7

3. Measure 5:

3. Takt 5:

3. Mesures 5:

Ab-7   D7   Db7   G7

4. Measure 7:

4. Takt 7:

4. Mesures 7:

Cø   Gb7   F7   B7b5

5. Measure 17:

5. Takt 17:

5. Mesures 17:

Cø   Gb7   F7   B7

6. Measure 19:

6. Takt 19:

6. Mesures 19:

Cø   Gb7   F7   B7

H. Substitutions are not used too much here, but there are a couple of places to try some simple, effective moves.

H. Substitutionen wurden bei dieser Aufnahme kaum verwendet. Es gibt aber ein paar Stellen, wo Sie einige einfache, effektive Akkordbewegungen probieren können.

H. Les substitutions ne sont pas employées beaucoup ici, mais il ya quelques endroits pour essayer certains mouvements simples mais efficaces.

1. Measure 5:

1. Takt 5:

1. Mesure 5:

2. Measure 16:

2. Takt 16:

2. Mesure 16:

3. Measure 17:

3. Takt 17:

3. Mesure 17:

I. In Art's solo (chorus I, M. 30) Victor and Rufus play a strong triplet figure. You might either play long, sustained voicings, or try one of these figures:

I. Während Art Farmers Solo (Chorus I, Takt. 30) spielen Victor Lewis und Rufus Reid markante Triolenfiguren. Sie können entweder lange gehaltene Voicings spielen, oder eine der folgenden Figuren probieren:

I. Dans le solo d' Art Farmer (structure I, mesure 30) Victor Lewis et Rufus Reid jouent une figure rythmique en triolets ayant beaucoup de force. Vous pouvez tout aussi bien jouer de longs accords soutenus, ou essayer quelques unes de ces figures rythmiques:

J. Here are some possible voicings for the Bb7b9sus4 in mm. 15 and 31:

J. Hier sind einige mögliche Voicings für den Akkord Bb7b9sus4 in den Takten 15 und 31.

J. Voici quelques harmonisations possibles pour l'accord de Bb7b9sus4 dans les mesures 15 et 31:

K. Try the technique of harmonizing a spontaneous background melody, discussed in "Karita" (Sugg. Ex. J). A possible melody for the first eight measures:

K. Versuchen Sie, eine spontane Background-Melodie zu harmonisieren, (siehe auch "Karita" - Übung J). Eine mögliche Melodie für die ersten acht Takte wäre:

K. Essayez la technique d'harmonisation spontanée d'une mélodie d'arrière plan sonore (contre-chant), discutée dans "Karita" (exercices suggérés J). Voici une mélodie pouvant être utilisée comme arrière-plan sonore, pour les huit premières mesures:

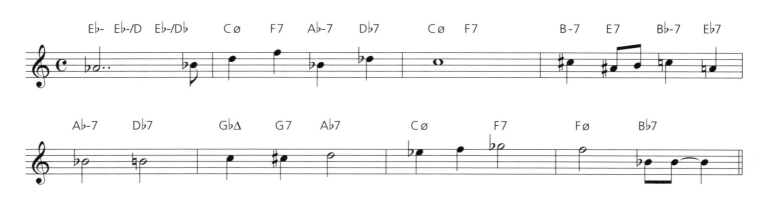

This melody might then be harmonized like this:

Diese Melodie könnte dann so harmonisiert werden:

Cette mélodie peut être harmonisée comme cela:

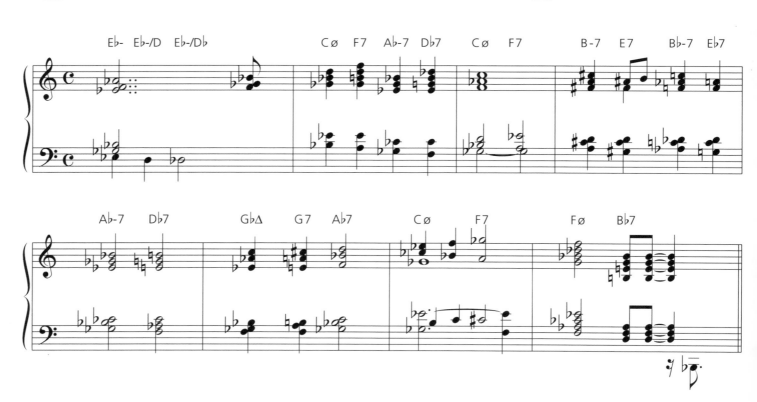

Robert Watson

KARITA

Robert Watson, Soloist

About The Tune:

This is a medium-tempo Latin (bossa-nova) tune. The form is AABA, with a bridge composed of three four-bar phrases. Total tune length is thirty-six measures. Bobby is the only soloist on the track. Note that the first two measures of the melody also serve as a 'send-off' into the first solo chorus. Alto solo is two choruses long.

About The Comping:

♦ Note the figures which the rhythm section plays in the head. They generally don't occur during the solo choruses.

♦ Although the rhythmic feel is derived from Latin-American music, the rhythm section does not play like a Latin-American group. We vary the rhythms, play off of each other, and create spontaneous figures, just as in any other jazz tune. We do, however, occasionally quote Latin rhythms (e. g. chorus II, mm. 1-4).

♦ There is little substitution.

♦ Rhythmically, the comping tends to be more active than it would be in a swing feel at this tempo.

♦ In a Latin tune the comping assumes a more percussive role. Think of the piano as a percussion instrument which is also capable of playing harmony. This percussive role is best achieved with definite, repetitive figures. The effect is strongest when the same voicing is used for each note of the figure.

♦ In the first chorus, the comping is more 'on the beat', in two-bar phrases. It also tends to 'energize' the second half of the second bar of the phrase, often with ♪ ♪ (e. g. chorus I, mm. 3-4)

Über das Stück:

Karita ist ein *medium-tempo Latin (bossa-nova)* Stück. Die Form ist AABA, wobei der Mittelteil in vier 4taktigen Phrasen komponiert wurde. Die Gesamtlänge des Stückes ist 36 Takte. Bobby Watson ist der einzige Solist dieser Aufnahme. Beachten Sie, daß die ersten zwei Takte der Melodie auch als *send-off* für den ersten Solochorus dienen. Das Altsolo ist zwei Chorusse lang.

Über die Begleitung:

♦ Achten Sie auf die Figuren, die die Rhythmusgruppe während des Melodieteils spielt.

♦ Obwohl der rhythmische Charakter von der lateinamerikanischen Musik stammt, spielt die Rhythmusgruppe nicht wie eine lateinamerikanische Gruppe. Wir variieren die Rhythmen, übernehmen Ideen voneinander und kreieren spontane Figuren, genau wie bei jedem anderen Jazzstück. Manchmal zitieren wir jedoch lateinamerikanische Rhythmen, so z.B. im zweiten Chorus, in den Takten 1-4.

♦ Es gibt wenig Substitution.

♦ Rhythmisch erscheint die Begleitung aktiver, im Gegensatz zu einem *Swing feel* in diesem Tempo.

♦ Bei einem Latin-Stück setzt die Begleitung eine perkussivere Rolle voraus. Stellen Sie sich das Klavier als ein Perkussionsinstrument vor, auf dem man auch Harmonien spielen kann. Diese perkussive Rolle kann am besten mit festgelegten, sich wiederholenden Figuren erfüllt werden. Der Effekt kann dadurch verstärkt werden, daß für jeden Ton der Figur das gleiche Voicing verwendet wird.

♦ Im ersten Chorus ist die Begleitung mehr auf dem Schlag, in 2taktigen Phrasen. Sie neigt außerdem dazu, der zweiten Hälfte des zweiten Taktes mehr 'Energie' zu geben, oft mit ♪ ♪ (Chorus I, Takte 3-4).

A propos du morceau:

Ceci est un morceau au tempo médium et de caractère afro-cubain (bossa nova). La forme est AABA, avec un "pont" (section B) composé de trois phrases de quatre mesures. La longueur totale du morceau est de trente six mesures. Bobby Watson est le seul soliste pour cette plage. Remarquez que les deux premières mesures de la mélodie servent aussi de mesures d'envoi, de "lanceur" à la premièr structure du solo.

A propos de l'accompagnement:

♦ Remarquez les figures rythmiques que la section rythmique joue pendant l'exposé du thème. On ne les retrouve pas, généralement, dans les structures des solos.

♦ Bien que le carctère rythmique provienne de la musique Latino-Américaine, la section rythmique ne joue pas comme un groupe Latino-Américain. Nous varions les rythmes, nous jouons les uns contre les autres et créons des figures rythmiques spontanément, comme dans n'importe quel thème de jazz. Nous faisons, cependant, de temps en temps, des citations de rythmes latins. (structure II, mesures 1-4).

♦ Il y a peu de substitutions.

♦ Rythmiquement, l'accompagnement tend à être beaucoup plus actif qu'il le serait dans un tempo à caractère "swing".

♦ Dans un morceau afro-cubain (Latin), l'accompagnement assume un rôle plus percussif. Pensez le piano comme un instrument de percussion qui est capable aussi de jouer une harmonie. Ce rôle percussif est beaucoup mieux réalisé avec des figures rythmiques bien définies et répétitives. L'effet est plus fort quand l'harmonisation utilisée est la même pour chaque note de la figure rythmique.

♦ Dans la première structure, l'accompagnement se place davantage sur le temps et dans des phrases de deux mesures. l'accompagnement tend à donner de l'énergie à la seconde moitié de la seconde mesure, enemployant souvent ce motif ♪ ♪ (structure I, mesure 3-4).

♦ The second chorus has larger voicings, more 'off the beat', starting with a typical samba rhythm:

♦ Im zweiten Chorus werden größere Voicings - mehr 'off the beat' [neben dem Schlag] verwendet - beginnend mit einem typischen Sambarhythmus:

♦ La deuxième structure possède des accords plus larges, placés davantage en dehors du temps et commençant avec un rythme typique de samba:

♦ The voicings in the second chorus are generally larger, to support the build in the alto solo. They come down near the end of his solo, to lead into the out head.

♦ Die Voicings im zweiten Chorus sind im allgemeinen größer, um so die Steigerung des Altsolos zu unterstützen. Sie nehmen gegen Ende des Solos ab und leiten in das Restatement der Melodie über.

♦ Les harmonisations dans la seconde structure sont généralement plus étendues, pour soutenir la montée de l'énergie dans le solo de sax-alto. Ces harmonisations diminuent d'intensité vers la fin de son solo, pour aboutir à l'exposition du thème final.

KARITA
Format

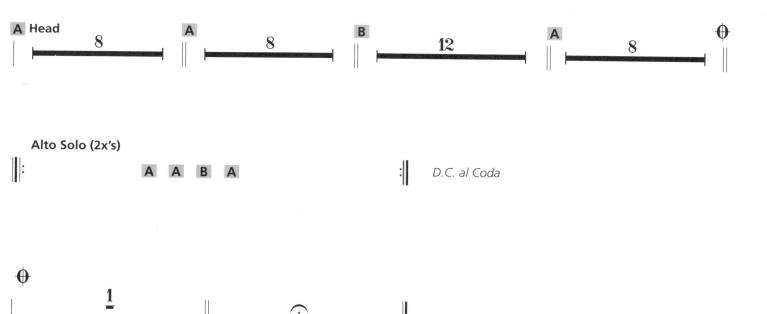

A Head   8   **A**   8   **B**   12   **A**   8

Alto Solo (2x's)

A **A** **B** **A**   *D.C. al Coda*

1

KARITA

Robert Watson

Solos

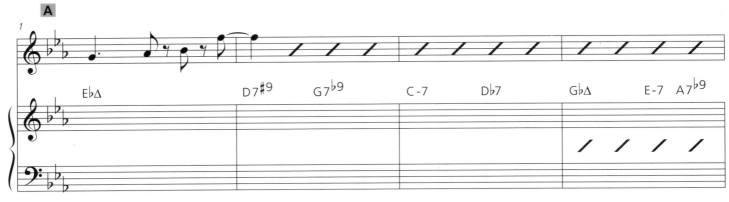

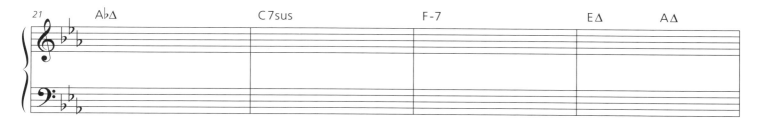

D.C. al Coda

Suggested Exercises:

A. 1. For Bobby Watson's solo, change the rhythmic nature every eight bars. For the first eight, use a lot of whole and half-note values, rolling some of the voicings. For the next eight, use lots of short, syncopated figures :

Suggested Exercises:

A. 1. Ändern Sie bei Bobby Watsons Solo die Rhythmik alle acht Takte. Verwenden Sie in den ersten acht Takten viele ganze und halbe Notenwerte, mit einigen arpeggierten Voicings. Benutzen Sie in den nächsten acht Takten viele kurze, synkopierte Figuren:

Exercices suggérés:

A. 1. Pour le solo de Bobby Watson, changez la nature rythmique toutes les huit mesures. Pour les huit premièrs, employez un nombre important de valeurs: rondes et blanches en faisant des roulements avec certains accords. Pour les huit mesures suivantes, employez un grand nombre de figures rythmiques courtes et syncopées:

For the bridge, try a "clave" pattern:

Probieren Sie im Mittelteil ein Clave-Motiv:

Pour le pond, (section B), essayez un motif de "clave":

For the last eight, go back to the long values. How, if at all, does each style affect the feel of the group? of the soloist? of the rhythm section?

2. Now try changing the sequence of comping styles: clave, long, "random", syncopated, clave. Does it make Bobby sound any different? How about the rest of the rhythm section?

3. Change the seuqence again: ask the same questions.

4. Now comp freely, in whatever way *you* think best serves the music. Why did you choose the technique(s) you chose? How does it (they) affect the soloist, the rhythm section, and the overall group?

B. Try some legato broken figures, especially on the bridge:

Kehren Sie in den letzten acht Takten wieder zu den langen Notenwerten zurück. Wie beeinflußt - falls überhaupt - jeder Stil den Charakter der Gruppe? des Solisten? der Rhythmusgruppe?

2. Ändern Sie nun die Reihenfolge des Begleitstils: Clave, lange Notenwerte, beliebig synkopiert, Clave. Klingt dadurch Bobby Watson anders? Oder der Rest der Rhythmusgruppe?

3. Ändern Sie die Reihenfolge noch einmal und stellen Sie sich dieselben Fragen.

4. Begleiten Sie als nächstes so, wie *Sie* denken, daß es der Musik am besten dient. Warum haben Sie sich für (eine) bestimmte Technik(en) entschieden? Welche Wirkung hat es auf den Solisten, die Rhythmusgruppe und auf die gesamte Gruppe?

B. Probieren Sie einige gebrochene Legato-Figuren aus, insbesondere im Mittelteil:

Pour les huit dernières mesures, retournez à des valeurs longues. Comment, si cela est, chaque style affecte-t-il le jeu d'ensemble du groupe? du soliste? de la section rythmique?

2. Maintenant essayez de changer le déroulement des styles d'accompagnement: clave, longues valeurs, syncopations au "hasard", clave. Est-ce-que cela fait sonner Bobby Watson différément? Et par rapport à la section rythmique? que se passe-t-il?

3. Changez de nouveau le cycle des différents styles; posez les mêmes questions.

4. Maintenant accompagnez librement, de la façon qui vous paraît être celle qui sert le mieux la musique. Pourquoi aviez vous choisi la/les technique(s) que vous avez choisi? De quelles façons elle, elles, affecte(nt) le soliste, la section rythmique, le groupe tout entier?

B. Essayez quelques figures rythmiques brisées mais liées, particulièrement sur le "pont" (section B).

C. You might try a montuno-like pattern, again on the bridge:

C. Sie können auch ein *montuno*-artiges Motiv im Mittelteil spielen.

C. Vous pouvez jouer un motif de style "montuno", une fois de plus sur le "pont":

D. Here is a combination of a samba pattern over a long guide-tone line:

D. Hier ist eine Kombination von Samba-Motiven über eine längere Leittonlinie:

D. Voici une combinaison d'un motif de samba au dessus d'une longue ligne guide:

E. Half-step embellishments of the chords can occasionally be effective. Here are a couple examples out of many possibilities:

E. Halbton-Umspielung der Akkorde kann gelegentlich effektiv sein. Hier sind ein paar Beispiele, von vielen möglichen:

E. Des embellissements d'accords réalisés avec des accords situés un demi-ton au dessus peuvent être de temps en temps efficaces. Voici quelques exemples parmi de nombreuses possibilités:

F. Try embellishing one-measure chords with diatonic motion:

F. Versuchen Sie eintaktige Akkorde mit diatonischer Bewegung auszuschmücken:

F. Essayez d'embellir les accords d'une mesure avec un mouvement diatonique:

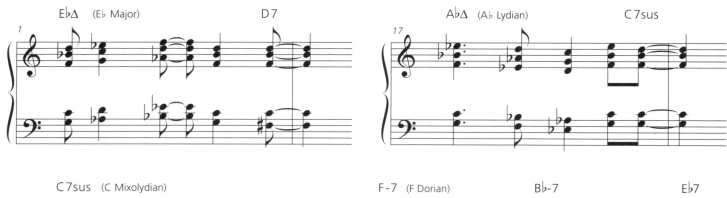

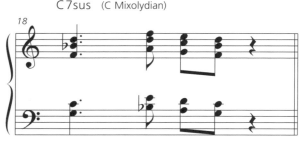

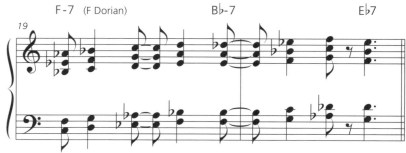

G. Where a diminished scale voicing is appropriate, try moving it in minor thirds:

G. Wo verminderte Skalen-Voicings passen, können Sie Bewegung in kleinen Terzen versuchen:

G. Quand une harmonisation avec la gamme diminuée est appropriée, essayez les mouvements en tierces mineures:

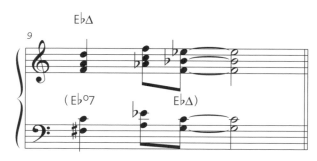

H. Here's another, different way to think of comping on a tune like Karita. The emphasis is on improvising a slow background melody, harmonizing it as you go. A suggested melody for the first eight bars might be:

H. Hier ist ein anderer Weg, an die Begleitung von "Karita" heranzugehen. Die Hauptsache dabei ist, eine langsame Background-Melodie zu improvisieren und sie spontan zu harmonisieren. Das folgende Beispiel zeigt eine Melodieempfehlung für die ersten acht Takte:

H. Voici une autre manière différente de penser pour accompagner un morceau comme "Karita". Mettre l'accent sur une mélodie improvisée se déroulant lentement, que vous harmonisez au fur et à mesure que vous avancez. Une mélodie suggérée pour ces huit premières mesures pourrait être:

Harmonized, this could be: Harmonisiert könnte das so aussehen: Harmonisée, cela pourra être:

Now write your own melody. Imagine it being played by a flugelhorn, or an alto saxophone. Harmonize it, using four- or five-note voicings. Play it along with the recording, reading if necessary. The more you do this, the more you'll start to be able to take your eyes off the paper, and *play the voicings as if you're improvising them.* Then you can start improvising harmonized background melodies *without* writing them out first.

I. There are a number of places for chromatic inner voice movement. A few examples:

Schreiben Sie als nächstes Ihre eigene Melodie. Stellen Sie sich vor, wie sie klingt, wenn sie von einem Flügelhorn oder einem Altsaxophon gespielt werden würde. Harmonisieren Sie sie mit vier- oder fünfstimmigen Voicings aus. Spielen Sie sie mit der Aufnahme, notfalls vom Notenblatt. Je mehr Sie das üben, desto häufiger werden Sie vom Notenblatt wegsehen und *die Voicings so spielen, als ob Sie improvisiert wären.* Nun können Sie harmonisierten Background improvisieren, *ohne* ihn zuerst zu notieren.

I. Es gibt eine Anzahl von Stellen für innere chromatische Bewegung. Hier ein paar Beispiele:

Maintenant écrivez votre propre mélodie. Imaginez qu'elle puisse être jouée par un flugelhorn (bugle) ou un saxophone alto. Harmonisez la, en vous servant d'accords à quatre ou cinq sons. Jouez-la avec l'enregistrement, en la lisant si cela est nécessaire. Au plus vous ferez cela et au plus vous commencerez à être capable de lever les yeux de la partition et de jouer les harmonisations *comme si vous les improvisiez.* Vous pourrez commencer à improviser des arrières-plans mélodiques, sans avoir à les écrire avant.

I. Il y a de nombreux endroits ou l'on peut avoir des lignes mélodiques se déplaçant chromatiquement à l'intérieur des voix. Voici quelques exemples:

J. Now relax, and comp along with the piano-less track using any of the techniques discussed in sections B through I. Repeat this several times. In a way, this is probably the most important exercise you'll do with this tune!

J. Begleiten Sie nun entspannt mit der klavierlosen Aufnahme und verwenden Sie dabei Techniken, die in B bis I besprochen wurden. Wiederholen Sie diesen Vorgang einige Male. Auf eine Art ist das wahrscheinlich die wichtigste Übung für dieses Stück!

J. Et maintenant détendez-vous, et accompagnez en vous servant de l'enregistrement ou le piano a ete enleve et en employant toutes les techniques discutées dans les sections B à I. Répétez cela plusieurs fois. D'une certaine façon, c'est probablement, l'exercice le plus important que vous allez faire avec ce morceau!

K. Finally, here are some larger voicings which you try on Karita. Group #1 employs upper-structure triads, while group #2 uses octave ("Red Garland") voicings.

K. Zum Schluß noch ein paar größere Voicings, die Sie zu "Karita" probieren können. Die erste Gruppe enthält sogenannte *upper-structure*-Dreiklänge, während die zweite Gruppe Oktav-Voicings ("Red Garland Voicings") verwendet.

K. Finalement, voici quelques harmonisations plus larges que vous pouvez essayer sur "Karita". Le groupe 1 emploie des structures supérieurs à trois sons pendant que le groupe 2 emploie des harmonisations en octaves à la Red Garland.

Triadic Upper Structures:

Upper Structures Dreiklänge:

Structures supérieures à triadiques:

Octave Voicings: **Oktav-Voicings:**   **Octave structures:**

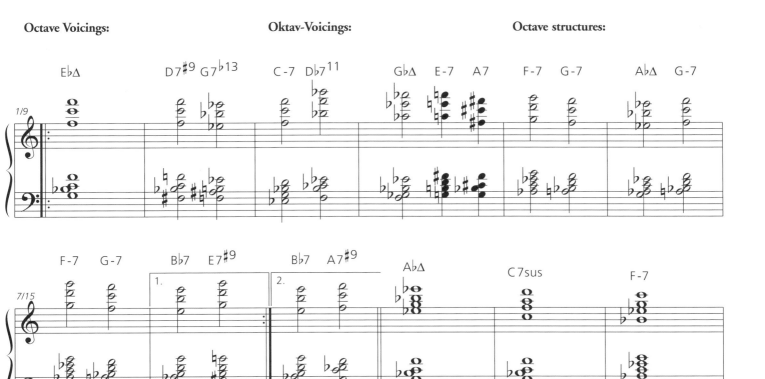

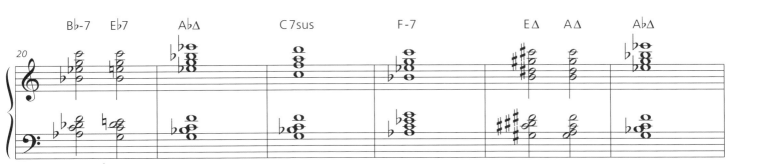

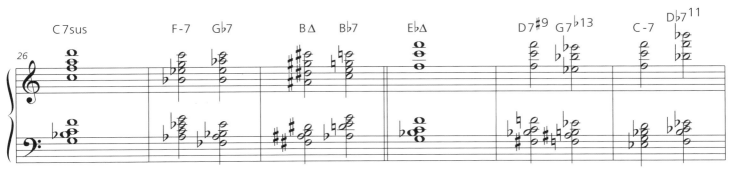

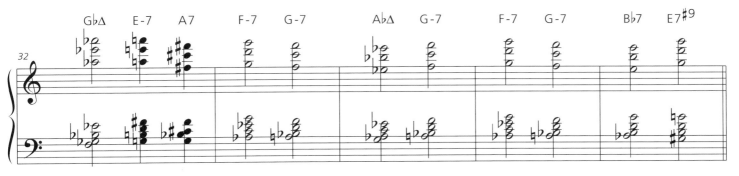

Jim McNeely
GIVE AND TAKE

Steve Erquiaga, Soloist

About The Tune:

Here is a 38-bar medium tempo tune which has four sections (A, B, C, & D). The harmony moves in a number of non-functional, surprising ways. It also uses pedals as key structural elements, similar to Herbie Hanccock's "Dolphin Dance". Solo order is Steve Erquiaga, guitar, for two choruses, and Rufus Reid, bass, for one.

About The Comping:

♦ The head has a number of figures played by the entire rhythm section (mm. 7-8, 14, 24, 28). These are occasionally played behind the soloist. By listening to each other, we could all 'feel' when the time was right to play one of the figures (e. g. chorus III, m. 28).

♦ The pedal sections of the tune have less sense of motion than do the non-functional, yet moving sections (e. g. mm. 7-8). These, in turn, have less motion than the places with *functional* harmony (mm. 11-12, 24-25 and 30-31). In general, progressions with little or no motion are more open to techniques which subdue or even eliminate the feeling of motion. These techniques include rolled chords, broken chords, use of the damper pedal to connect or blend two or more voicings for the same chord, upper-register splashes, and diatonic embellishment of a voicing. The comping in the 4/4, walking sections usually employs direct, single attacks.

♦ The underlying 'feel' shifts throughout the performance. At various times the rhythm section is in a '2' feel, walking '4', straight eighth note, broken '2', and double time. In the '2' feel, the comping tends to be less active, then the voicings are held for a longer duration, than in the '4'. The transitions from one feel to another are made smoothly, usually starting a bar or two before the next section actually begins. All of these changes in feel were done spontaneously, with no discussion before-hand.

♦ There is a strong implication of triplets in the comping, especially in the pedal sections.

♦ The comping helps maintain the flow of energy going into the bass solo. Also note how

Über das Stück:

Hier ist ein 38taktiges Stück in einem medium Tempo, das aus vier Teilen (A, B, C & D) besteht. Die Harmonik bewegt sich auf einer Vielzahl von nichtfunktionalen, überraschenden Wegen. Zudem wird Orgelpunkt als strukturales Element eingesetzt, ähnlich wie bei Herbie Hancocks "Dolphin Dance". Die Reihenfolge der Soli: Steve Erquiaga - Gitarre, zwei Chorusse und Rufus Reid - Baß, ein Chorus.

Über die Begleitung:

♦ Der Melodieteil enthält eine Reihe von Figuren, die von der gesamten Rhythmus-gruppe gespielt werden (Takte 7-8, 14, 24, 28). Sie werden gelegentlich hinter dem Solisten gespielt. Weil wir aufeinander hörten, konnten wir alle 'spüren', wann der richtige Zeitpunkt war, eine dieser Figuren zu spielen (z. B. Chorus III, Takt 28).

♦ Die Orgelpunktbereiche des Stückes haben weniger Bewegung als die nichtfunktionalen, aber trotzdem bewegten Teile (z.B. Takte 7-8). Diese haben wiederum weniger Bewegung als die Bereiche mit *funktionaler* Harmonik (Takte 11-12, 24-25 und 30-31). Im allgemeinen sind Progressionen mit wenig, oder überhaupt keiner Bewegung offener für Techniken, die sich der Bewegung unter-werfen oder das Bewegungsgefühl gänzlich unterbinden. Diese Techniken schließen abgerollte Akkorde, gebrochene Akkorde, Verwendung des Dämpfpedals zur Verbin-dung von zwei oder mehr Voicings für ein-und denselben Akkord, 'Farbtupfer' im hohen Register und diatonische Umspielung eines Voicings mit ein. Während der 4/4 *walking* Bereiche werden für die Begleitung direkte, einfache Anschläge verwendet.

♦ Der zugrundeliegende Charakter wechselt während der gesamten Aufnahme. Zu unter-schiedlichen Zeiten spielt die Rhythmus-gruppe in einem *2-feel,* in *walking 4,* in gleichmäßigen Achteln [binär], in *broken 2* und in *double time.* Während des *2-feels* neigt die Begleitung zu weniger Aktivität und die Voicings werden länger ausgehalten als in den

A propos du morceau:

Voici un morceau de trente huit mesures de tempo médium qui comporte quatre sections mélodiques (A, B, C, et D). L'harmonie se déplace un certain nombre de fois de manière surprenante et non fonctionelle. Il emploie aussi des pédales comme des éléments structurels de tonalité, similaires à celles employées par Herbie Hancock dans "Dolphin Dance". L'ordre des solos est Steve Erquiaga, guitar, pour deux structures et Rufus Reid, basse, pour une structure.

A propos de l'accompagnement:

♦ L'exposé du theme d'ouverture comporte un nombre de figures rythmiques joué par la section rythmique entière (mesures 7-8, 14, 24, 28). Elles seront employées occasio-nellement derrière le soliste. En s'écoutant les uns les autres, nous "sentirons" le bon moment pour jouer une de ces figures. (Exemple: structure III, mesure 28).

♦ Les sections comportant une pédale donnent une impression de mouvement moins important que les sections comportant des harmonies non-fonctionelles et pourtant pleines de mouvement (voir les mesures 7-8). Celles-ci, en fin de compte, ont moins de mouvement que les endroits ayant une harmonie *fonctionelle* (mesures 11-12, 24-25 et 30-31). En général, des progressions avec peu ou sans mouvement sont plus ouverts à des techniques qui atténuent ou même éliminent le sentiment de mouvement. Ces techniques incluent des accords roulés, des accords brisés*, l'emploi de la pédale étouffoir pour relier ou mélanger deux ou plusieurs harmonisations du même accord, des séries de sons dans le registre aigu (appelées "éclaboussures" de sons) et des embellisse-ments diatoniques d'une harmonisation ou accord. l'accompagnement dans les sections à 4 temps et ayant un mouvement de swing évident emploie généralement des attaques directes et uniques.

*Broken chords: Ce sont des accords dont toutes les parties ne sont pas émises simultanément mais rythmiquement l'une après l'autre.

Steve's triplet figure in mm. 32-33 of chorus II is picked up in the piano in m. 35 ; then Rufus uses the triplet idea to start his own solo.

♦ Dynamic shading plays a very important part in comping on this tune. This applies not only to the piano, but to all members of the rhythm section.

♦ The comping contains a wide variety of sizes of voicings.

♦ Little, if any substitution occurs in the harmony (see "Crossroads", "About The Comping"). This is due to the already complex nature of the tune's harmony as originally written.

4/4 *walking* Bereichen. Der Übergang von einem Teil zum anderen erfolgt reibungslos. In der Regel beginnt er ein oder zwei Takte vor vor dem nächsten Teil. All diese Wechsel sind spontan passiert, ohne vorherige Absprache.

♦ In die Begleitung werden ausgiebig Triolen einbezogen, ganz besonders in den Bereichen mit Orgelpunkt.

♦ Die Begleitung trägt dazu bei, daß der Energiefluß auf dem Weg in das Baßsolo nicht abreißt. Beachten Sie außerdem, wie Steve Erquiagas Triolenfigur in den Takten 32-33 des zweiten Chorus vom Klavier in Takt 35 aufgegriffen wird. Rufus Reid verwendet diese Triolenidee für den Anfang seines eigenen Solos.

♦ Dynamische Schattierungen spielen bei der Begleitung dieses Stückes eine wichtige Rolle. Das gilt nicht nur für das Piano, sondern für die gesamte Rhythmusgruppe.

♦ Die Begleitung enthält eine Vielfalt unterschiedlich gewichteter Voicings.

♦ Die Harmonik enthält wenig Substitutionen. (siehe "Crossroads", "Über die Begleitung"). Das kommt daher, da das Stück selbst harmonisch komplex ist.

♦ Le "caractère" sous-jacent change tout au long de l'éxécution du morceau. A différents moments la section rythmique joue en donnant l'impression d'un tempo à "deux temps", puis d'un tempo swingué à 4 temps, et ensuite en croches égales (binaire), tempo brisés à 2 temps, et tempos doublés. Dans le tempo ayant un caractère à 2 temps, l'accompagnement tend à être moins actif, les harmonisations sont jouée avec des durées plus longues qu'en 4/4. Les transitions entre les sections de caractère différent sont faites sans heurt, commençant habituellement une ou deux mesures avant que la section suivante commence. Tous ces changements de caractère furent fait spontanément, sans en avoir discuté avant de jouer.

♦ Il y a une très forte implication des triolets dans l'accompagnement, et particulièrement dans les sections où l'on emploie les pédales.

♦ l'accompagnement aide à maintenir le flot d'énergie allant dans le solo de basse. Remarquez aussi comment la figure rythmique en triolets de Steve Erquiaga dans les mesures 32-33 de la deuxième structure est captée par le piano dans la mesures 35; Puis Rufus Reid emploie une idée en triolets pour commencer son propre solo.

♦ Les nuances jouent un rôle très important dans l'accompagnement de ce morceau. Ceci s'applique non seulement au piano, mais à tous les membres de la section rythmique.

♦ L'accompagnement contient une large variété de dimensions dans les harmonisations.

♦ Trés peu, voire même aucune substitution ne se produit dans l'harmonie (voir "Crossroads", "à propos de l'accompagnement"). Ceci est dû à la nature déjà complexe de l'harmonie de ce morceau telle qu'elle a été originellement écrite.

GIVE AND TAKE
Format

A Head ‖: 16 ‖ **B** 8 ‖ **C** 6 ‖ **D** 8 ⊕ ‖

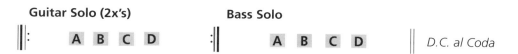

Guitar Solo (2x's) ‖: **A** **B** **C** **D** :‖ **Bass Solo** **A** **B** **C** **D** ‖ *D.C. al Coda*

⊕ **(2x's)** ‖: 4 ⌢ ‖ :‖

GIVE AND TAKE

Jim McNeely

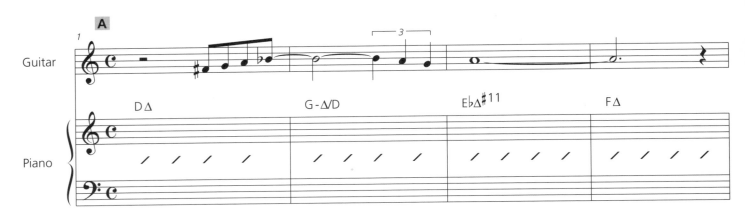

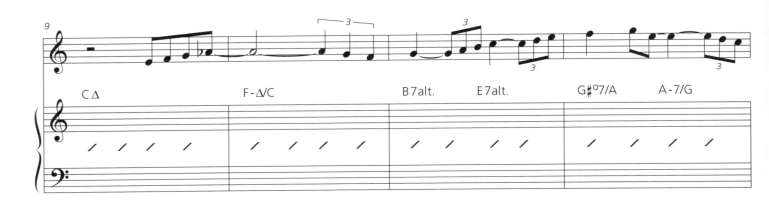

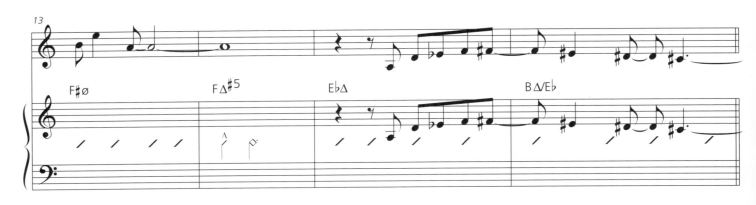

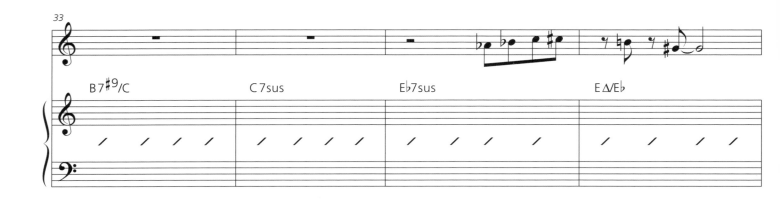

to solos

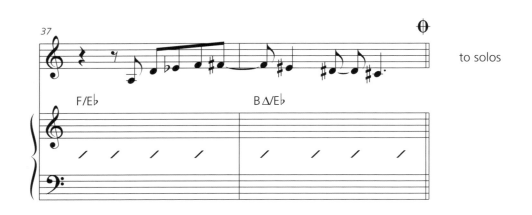

Solos:

A   "2-feel" or "walk"

1 DΔ   G-Δ/D   EbΔ   FΔ

5 GΔ   C-Δ/G   AbΔ A7b13   BbΔ B7b5

9 CΔ   F-Δ/C   B7alt. E7alt.   G#°7/A A-7/G

13 F#ø   FΔ#5   EbΔ   BΔ/Eb

B

17 DΔ   D7¹¹   DΔ#5   E/D

C

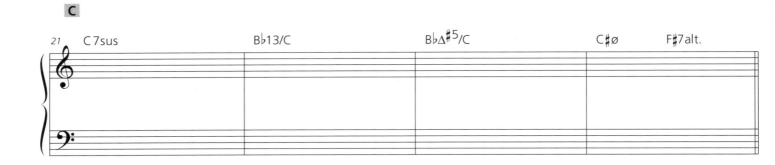

21 C7sus   Bb13/C   BbΔ#5/C   C#ø   F#7alt.

"Walk"

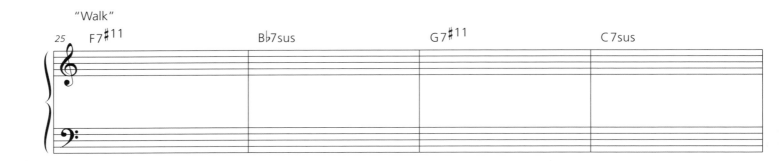

25 F7#11   Bb7sus   G7#11   C7sus

D "Pedal"

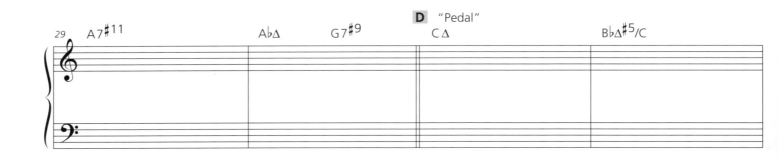

29 A7#11   AbΔ   G7#9   CΔ   BbΔ#5/C

33 B7#9/C   C7sus   Eb7sus   EΔ/Eb

37 F/Eb   BΔ/Eb

after solos D.C. al Coda

Suggested Exercises:

A. The solo section for "Give And Take" indicates the different feels played by the rhythm section on the recording. Practice thinking ahead so that you suggest the new feel two to four beats before it actually begins.

B. At this tempo, a chord which lasts a full measure may usually be embellished with the chord a half-step above. In the first sixteen bars alone you might try this in mm. 1, 3, 4, 5, 9, 13, 14, 15, and 16. A couple of examples:

Empfohlene Übungen:

A. Im Soloteil von "Give And Take" sind die unterschiedlichen *feels,* die von der Rhythmusgruppe bei der Aufnahme gespielt wurden, gekennzeichnet. Üben Sie voraus-zudenken, damit Sie das neue *feel,* zwei bis vier Takte, bevor es eigentlich beginnt, anregen können.

B. Bei diesem Tempo kann ein Akkord, der einen ganzen Takt dauert, mit dem Akkord, der einen Halbtonschritt darüber liegt, umspielt werden. Schon in den ersten 16 Takten können Sie das in den Takten 1, 3, 4, 5, 9, 13, 14, 15 und 16 ausprobieren. Hier ein paar Beispiele:

Exercices suggérés:

A. La section solo pour "Give And Take" indique les parties de caractère différent jouées par la section rythmique sur l'enregistrement. Travaillez en pensant à l'avance, de telle façon que vous puissiez suggérer le caractère nouveau de la section suivante deux ou quatre temps avant qu'elle ne commence réellement.

B. A ce tempo, un accord qui dure une mesure complete peut généralement être embelli, par l'accord situé un demi-ton au dessus. Dans les seize premières mesures seulement vous pouvez essayer cela dans les mesures 1, 3, 4, 5, 9, 13, 14, 15, et 16. Quelques exemples:

C. There are a couple of instances where you might insert a chromatic passing chord:

   1. Measures 3 and 4:

C. Es gibt ein paar Stellen, wo Sie einen chromatischen Durchgangsakkord einfügen können:

   1. Takte 3 und 4:

C. Il y a quelques circonstances ou vous pourrez insérer un accord de passage chromatique:

   1. Mesures 3 et 4:

   2. Measure 27:

   2. Takt 27:

   2. Mesure 27:

D. The medium tempo, whole-note harmonic rhythm, and non-functional harmony of this tune afford a number of places to use diatonic embellishment of the chords. Here are four typical examples:

D. Das medium Tempo, die Bereiche mit ganz-taktigem harmonischem Rhythmus und mit nichtfunktionaler Harmonik, bieten eine Reihe von Stellen für die Verwendung diatonischer Umspielung der Akkorde. Hier sind vier typische Beispiele:

D. Le tempo médium, le rythme harmonique en ronde et l'harmonie non fonctionelle de ce morceau, tout cela fournit un certain nombre d'endroits où l'on peut employer un embellissement diatonique des accords. Voici quatre exemples caractèristiques:

E. Here are some broken patterns to practice (slowly at first). Apply them to the appropriate pedal part of the tune:

E. Hier sind einige Motive mit gebrochenen Akkorden - zum Üben (zuerst langsam). Wenden Sie sie bei den entsprechenden Orgelpunktbereichen dieses Stückes an:

E. Voici quelques motifs "brisés" (motifs à la fois rythmiques et harmoniques "partagés" entre les 2 mains) à travailler (lentement d'abord). Appliquez les à la partie appropriée du morceau, employant une note pédale.

F. Sample voicings: Here are some different ways to voice selected segments of "Give and Take". Note that with chords over a different bass note (slash chords), often times the bass note may be omitted from the piano voicing.

F. Vorschläge für Voicings: Hier sind einige unterschiedliche Voicings für bestimmte Bereiche von "Give and Take". Beachten Sie, daß bei Akkorden mit einem anderen Baßton (slash chords), häufig der Baßton beim Piano-Voicing weggelassen werden kann.

F. Exemples d'harmonisations: Voici différentes façons d'harmoniser des fragments choisis de "Give and Take". Remarquez qu'avec les accords qui ont une note de basse différente de leur nom*, la note de basse peut souvent être supprimée de l'harmonisation de l'accord de piano.

*Slash chords: Ces accords sont des accords ècrits sur une basse différentes du nom de l'accord: exemple B♭△/E♭ (basse).

Give And Take   73

Jim McNeely

LAST MINUTE

Steve Erquiaga, Soloist

About The Tune:

This is an up-tempo tune with 'modal' harmony. The harmonic rhythm of eight measures per chord gives the player an opportunity to really explore the scale associated with each of those chords. The form is AA'BA, with the bridge being sixteen measures. This adds up to a fourty-bar tune.

If you find it difficult to keep up with the fast tempo, don't worry, you're not alone! Try feeling the tempo in half-notes (1-3-1-3), or even whole notes (1-1-1-1). The only soloist on this track is guitarist Steve Erquiaga, who plays four choruses.

About The Comping:

♦ The comping in this tune relies on *pandiatonicism:* the scale associated with each chord generates most of the primary and passing voicings used. The long harmonic rhythm of "Last Minute" gives you a chance to really utilize this technique. Here are the chord/scale relationships:

Über das Stück:

"Last Minute" ist ein *up-tempo* Stück mit 'modaler' Harmonik. Der harmonische Rhythmus, mit je acht Takten pro Akkord, gibt dem Musiker die Möglichkeit, die zu diesen Akkorden passenden Skalen ausgiebig zu erkunden. Die Form ist AA'BA, mit einem 16taktigen Mittelteil und insgesamt 40 Takten.

Sollte es Ihnen schwer fallen, mit dem schnellen Tempo Schritt zu halten, ärgern Sie sich nicht, sie sind nicht allein! Versuchen Sie das Tempo in Halben zu spüren (1-3, 1-3), oder sogar in Ganzen (1-1-1-1). Der einzige Solist dieser Aufnahme ist Steve Erquiaga, er spielt vier Chorusse.

Über die Begleitung:

♦ Die Begleitung dieses Stückes stützt sich auf *Pandiatonik:* Die Skala, die mit dem Akkord korrespondiert, liefert die meisten Haupt- und Durchgangs-Voicings, die hier verwendet wurden. Der lange harmonische Rhythmus von "Last Minute" ermöglicht Ihnen, diese Technik nutzbar zu machen. Das folgende Beispiel zeigt das Akkord/Skalenverhältnis:

A propos du morceau:

C'est un morceau au tempo très rapide avec une harmonie "modale". Le rythme harmonique de huit mesures pour un accord donne au musicien l'occasion de réllement explorer la gamme associée avec chacun de ces accords. La forme est AA'BA, avec l "pont" (section B) comptant seize mesures. Ce qui donne un morceau de 40 mesures.

Si vous trouvez difficile de suivre le tempo rapide, ne vous inquiétez pas, vous n'êtes pas seul! Essayez de ressentir le tempo en blanches (1-3-1-3) ou même en rondes (1-1-1-1). Le seul soliste sur cette plage enregistrée est le guitariste Steve Erquiaga, qui joue 4 structures.

A propos de l'accompagnement:

♦ l'accompagnement dans ce morceau s'appuie sur la *pan-diatonicité:* La gamme associée à chaque accord génère la plupart des accords de base et des accords de passage employés. Le rythme harmonique de longue durée de "Last Minute" vous donne une chance d'utiliser réellement cette technique. Voici les relations entre la gamme et l'accord:

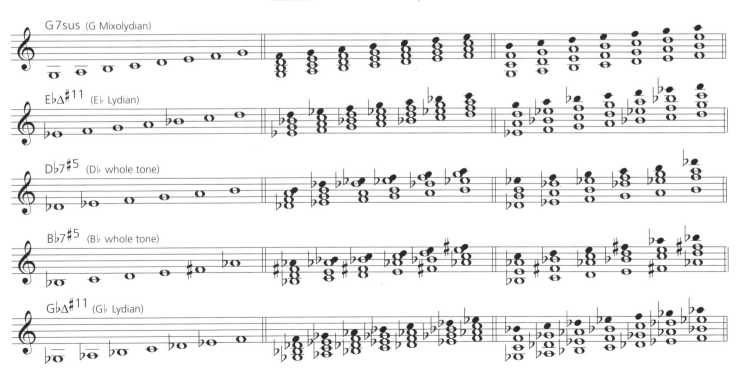

- In comping pan-diatonically, it is even more important to consider the melody of the comping. This helps to give the comping a better sense of direction through the eight-bar phrases.

- The comping on the first head chorus uses small voicings, and simple rhythmic patterns. On the out chorus, the comping is much more active; it utilizes larger, more powerful voicings, as well. This contributes to the overall effect that, after the energy of the solo, the out head wants to retain some of that energy, and not go back to its original state.

- The only pre-conceived rhythmic figure is the 'hit' on '4-and' of measure 30. This usually occurs during each solo chorus, and functions as a target point at the end of the bridge.

- During the solo the bridge (m. m. 17-32) tends to get rhythmically broken up much more than the other sections of the tune.

- The Tyner-esque left hand root and fifth voicings helps to 'anchor' the harmony. This anchor usually prepares the way for increased diatonic or chromatic activity.

- Listen for the effect of the rhythmic figure at the very end of the second solo chorus 𝄞. It both fills the hole in the solo, and helps to propel the group into the next chorus.

- The comping gets really chromatic only at two different places. At the end of the first chorus the chromaticism creates tension while leading into the second chorus. And in the third chorus, the chromaticism in the E♭Δ section helps to provide contrast to the repeated pattern in the guitar solo.

- Bei der pandiatonischen Begleitung ist es noch wichtiger, die Melodie, die sich aus ihr ergibt, zu berücksichtigen. Das hilft, daß im Verlauf der achttaktigen Phrasen besser zu erkennen ist, in welche Richtung sich die Begleitung bewegt.

- Die Begleitung des Melodieteils verwendet kleinere Voicings und einfache rhythmische Motive. Während des Melodie-Restatements ist sie wesentlich aktiver und es werden zudem größere, kraftvollere Voicings verwendet. Das trägt dazu bei, daß das Melodie-Restatement etwas von der Energie des Solos beibehält und nicht zum Ausgangspunkt zurückkehrt.

- Die einzige, vorher festgelegte rhythmische Figur ist der 'Schlag' auf '4und' in Takt 30. In der Regel kommt das in jedem Solochorus vor, und hat die Funktion eines Zielpunktes am Ende des Mittelteils.

- Während des Solos neigt der Mittelteil (Takte 17-32) zu mehr rhythmischer Freizügigkeit *(broken time)*, viel mehr als die anderen Teile dieses Stückes.

- Tonika-Quint-Voicings à la McCoy Tyner helfen, die Harmonie zu 'verankern'. Dieser Anker ist im allgemeinen der Wegbereiter für verstärkte diatonische oder chromatische Aktivität.

- Hören Sie auf den Effekt dieser rhythmischen Figur am Ende des zweiten Solochorus': 𝄞. Sie füllt eine Pause des Solos und hilft, die Gruppe in den nächsten Chorus zu befördern.

- Nur an zwei verschiedenen Stellen wird die Begleitung wirklich chromatisch. Am Ende des ersten Chorus' wird durch Chromatik Spannung erzeugt, während sie in den zweiten Chorus überleitet. Und im dritten Chorus sorgt Chromatik für Kontrast gegenüber dem wiederholten Motiv des Gitarrensolos.

- En accompagnant d'une façon pandiatonique il est extrêmement important de considérer la mélodie formée par l'accompagnement. Ceci aide à donner à l'accompagnement un meilleur sens de la direction que l'on suit pendant les phrases de huit mesures.

- L'accompagnement sur la première structure d'exposition du thème emploie des accords peu fournis et des motifs rythmiques simples. Sur la structure d'exposition finale du thème l'accompagnement est beaucoup plus actif; il utilise des accords plus larges et plus puissants à la fois. Ceci contribue à l'amélioration de l'impression d'ensemble, en effet: après l'énergie importante degagée dans le solo, l'exposition du thème final à besoin de retenir une partie de cette énergie et de ne pas retourner à la manière utilisée pour la première exposition du thème.

- La seule figure rythmique prédéterminée employée est le coup donné sur la deuxième partie du quatrième temps de la mesure 30 (le "4et"). Ceci se répète dans chaque structure des solos, et fonctionne comme un point cible à la fin du "pont" (section B).

- Durant les solos le "pont" (section B, mesures 17-32) tend à être rythmiquement plus "cassé", "brisé" que les autres sections du morceau; (plus linéaires).

- L'emploi à la main gauche de la fondamentale et de la quinte "à la McCoy Tyner" aide à "ancrer", fixer l'harmonie. Cet "ancrage" prépare générale-ment la voie à une activité diatonique et chromatique accrue.

- Ecoutez l'effet produit par la figure rythmique à la fin de la seconde structure de solo 𝄞. Ce rythme joue deux rôles, il remplit l'espace laissé vide par le soliste et il aide à propulser le groupe dans la nouvelle structure.

- L'accompagnement ne devient réellement chromatique qu'à deux endroits différénts. A la fin de la première structure le chromatisme crée une tension pour aboutir dans la deuxième structure. Et dans la troisième structure, le chromatisme de la section en Mi♭Δ aide à fournir le contraste à un motif répétitif dans du solo de guitare.

LAST MINUTE
Format

A Head | 8 | **A'** | 8 | **B** | 16 | **A** | 8

Guitar Solo (4x's)

A **A'** **B** **A**   *D.C. al Coda*

7

LAST MINUTE

Jim McNeely

Solo: (4 choruses)

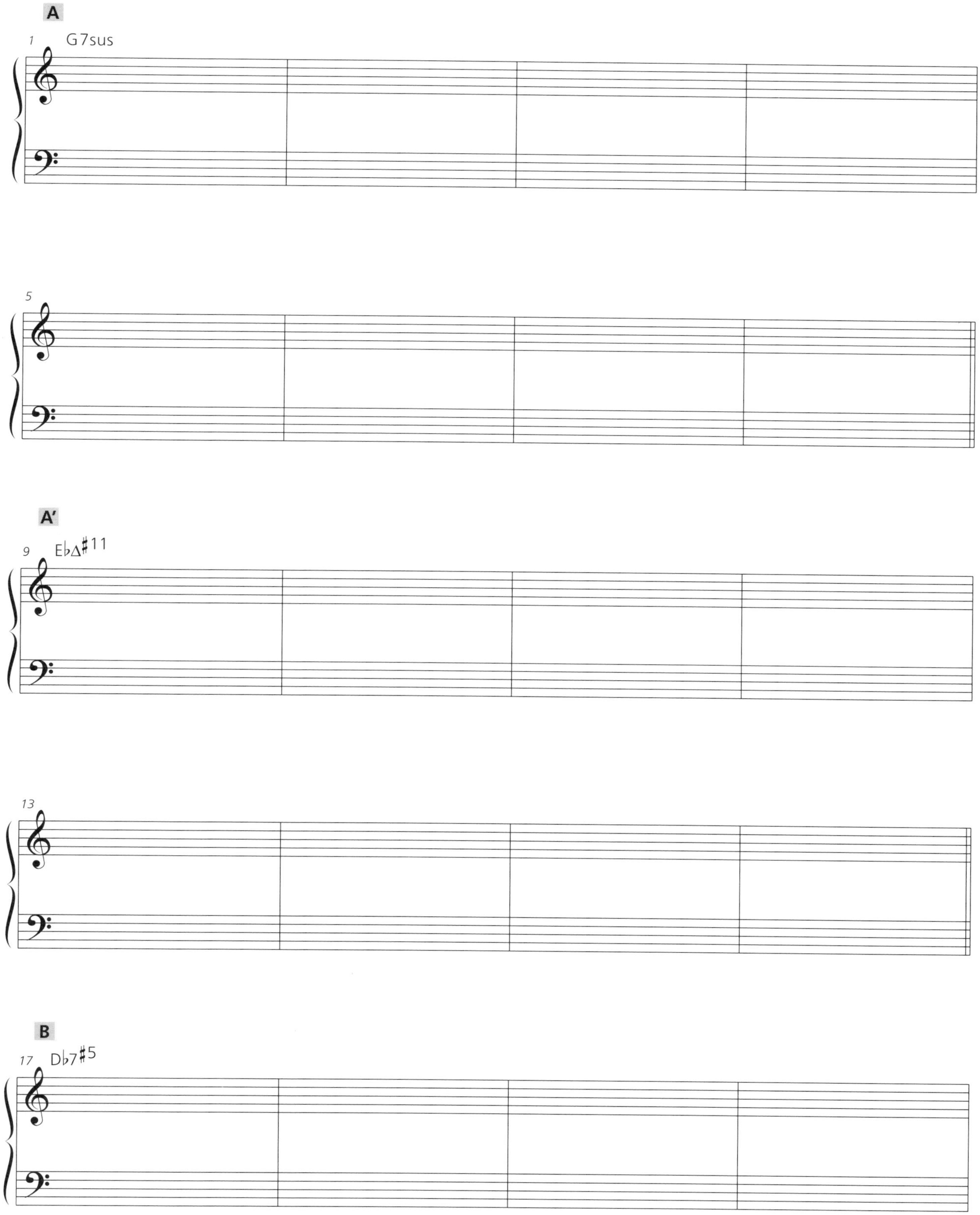

A

1 G7sus

5

A'

9 E♭△♯11

13

B

17 D♭7♯5

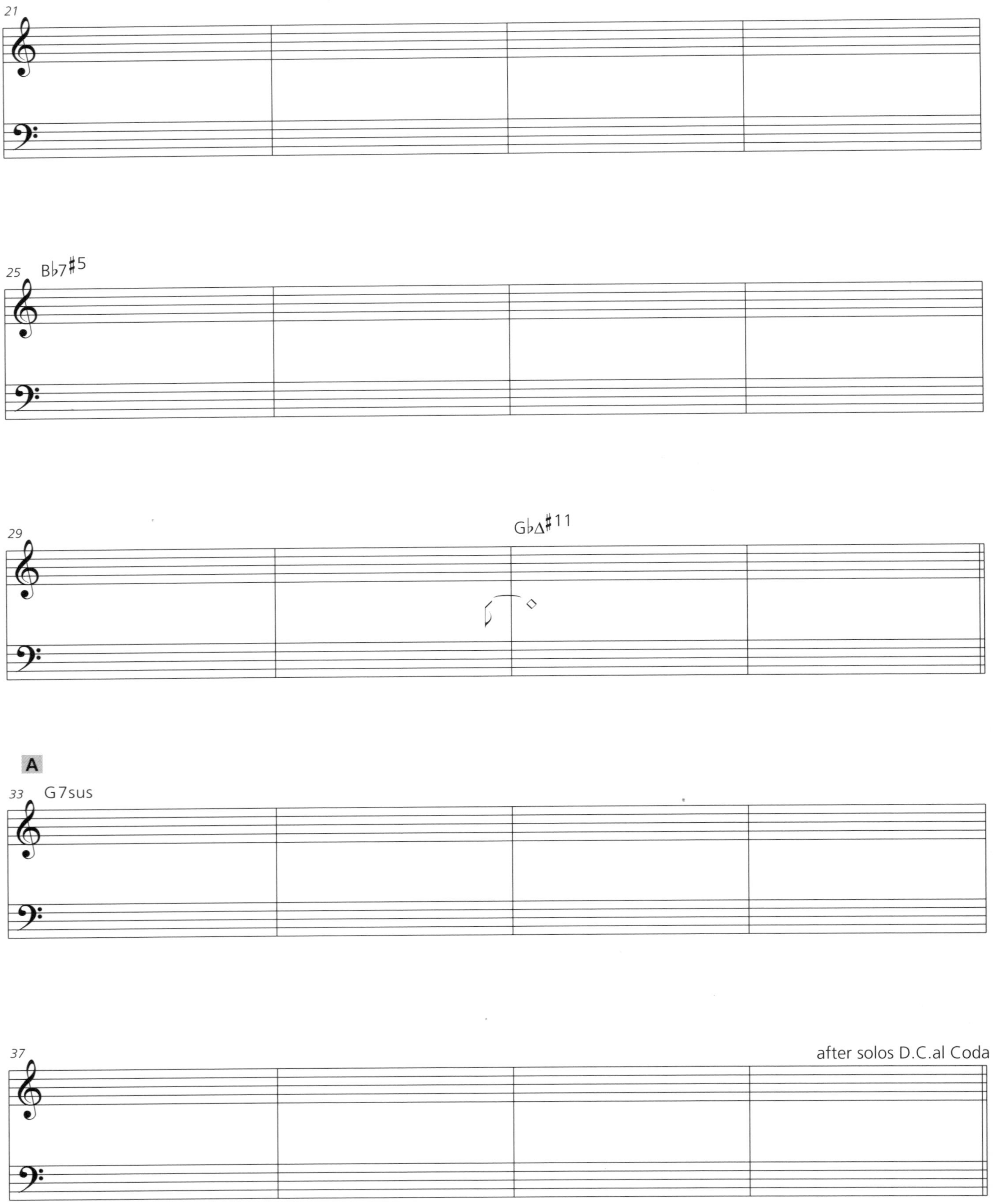
21
25
B♭7♯5
29
G♭∆♯11
A
33
G7sus
37
after solos D.C.al Coda

Suggested Exercises:

A. Here are some sample voicings for each of the chords of "Last Minute". For the 7sus4 and $\Delta^{\sharp 11}$ chords there are several groupings of voicings, according to how they are constructed: quartal (based on fourth), inverted quartals (e. g. 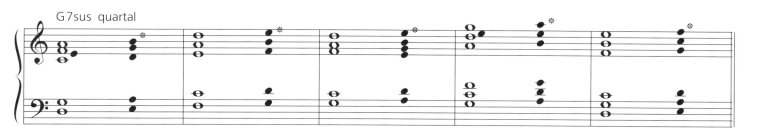 is inverted to form 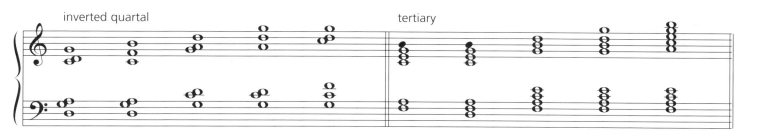) tertiary (based on thirds), combination (based on thirds and fourth), and octave (using an octave in the right hand). Note that the quartal voicings have upper neighbor voicings*, which can be freely used to create more motion in your comping, as well as to create vamps. The $7^{\sharp 5}$ chords are limited to tertiary and octave voicings.

Empfohlene Übungen:

A. Hier sind einige Voicing-Beispiele für jeden einzelnen Akkord von "Last Minute". Für die 7sus4 und $\Delta^{\sharp 11}$ Akkorde gibt es mehrere Gruppen von Voicings, unterteilt nach ihrem Aufbau: in Quarten, in umgekehrten Quarten (z. B. aus wird umgekehrt), in Terzen, in Kombinationen von Terzen und Quarten und in Oktav-Voicings (mit der rechten Hand wird eine Oktave gespielt). Beachten Sie, daß die Quarten-Voicings die darüberliegenden Nachbar-Voicings* enthalten. Sie können dazu verwendet werden, mehr Bewegung in Ihrer Begleitung zu erzeugen und für Vamps. Die $7^{\sharp 5}$ Akkorde beschränken sich auf Terz- und Oktav-Voicings.

Exercices suggérés:

A. Voici quelques exemples d'harmonisations pour chacun des accords de "Last Minute". Pour les accords de 7sus4 et $\Delta^{\sharp 11}$ il y a plusieurs groupements d'harmonisations, correspondants à la façon dont ils sont construits: "quartal" (basés sur les quartes). "Quartal inversé" (par exemple est inversé pour formér), "tertiaire" (basé sur les tierces), "combinée" (basés sur les tierces et les quartes), et "d'octave" (employant une octave à la main droite). Remarquez que les harmonisations quartales ont des harmonisations voisines* supérieures pouvant être employées librement dans votre accompagnement pour créer plus de mouvement; et aussi créer des "obstinati", (vamp = obstinato). Les accords $7^{\sharp 5}$ sont limités aux harmonisations "tertiaires" et "d'octave".

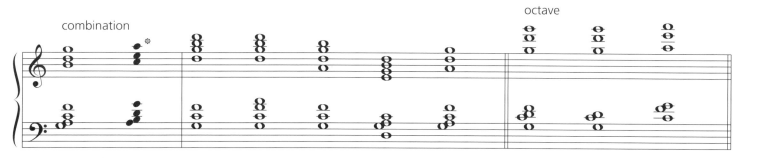

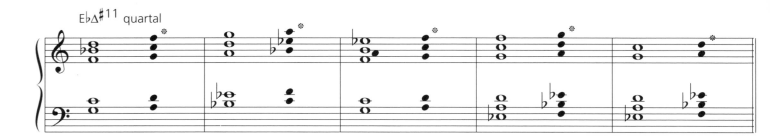

Most of these voicings may be played a minor third higher for G♭Δ♯11.

Die meisten dieser Voicings können für G♭Δ♯11 um eine kleine Terz höher gespielt werden.

La plupart de ces harmonisations peuvent être jouées une tierce mineure au dessus pour Sol♭Δ♯11.

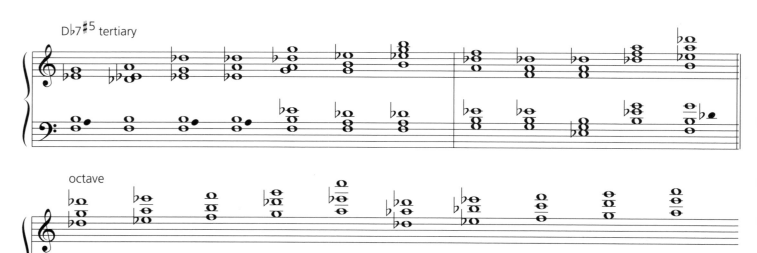

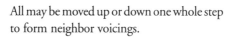 possible left hand structures

All may be moved up or down one whole step to form neighbor voicings.

Most of these voicings may be played a minor third lower for B♭7♯5.

Alle Voicings können zur Bildung von Nachbar-Voicings um einen Ganzton nach oben oder unten transponiert werden.

Die meisten dieser Voicings können für B♭7♯5 um eine kleine Terz tiefer gespielt werden.

Toutes ces harmonisations peuvent être montées ou descendues d'un ton pour former des harmonisations voisines.

La plupart de ces harmonisations peuvent être jouées une tierce mineure au dessus pour Si♭7♯5.

You might try several ideas for practicing these voicings:

1. Write out voicings for a whole chorus, using one voicing per chord. Use voicings of similar size, density, and location on the keyboard.

2. Do #1 several times, making sure that each time the size, density, and location of the voicings for each chord are similar.

3. Write voicings for an entire chorus, using groups of two, three, or four voicings from each group for each chord.

4. Write voicings for four choruses. Start with small voicings in the first chorus, move to larger ones in the second, even larger ones in the third, and octave voicings in the fourth.

For each of these exercises, you may want to first practice the voicings slowly, without the recording. A metronome or drum machine may also be used while you practice. Once you've gotten the voicings near the tempo of the recording, try playing them along with the pre-recorded track.

B. One effective way to comp in a modal tune is to create simple vamps, using a quartal voicing and its neighbor. Here are few examples:

Sie können beim Üben dieser Voicings mehrere Ideen ausprobieren:

1. Notieren Sie Voicings für einen ganzen Chorus - ein Voicing pro Akkord. Benutzen Sie Voicings mit ähnlicher Größe, Dichte und Lage auf der Tastatur.

2. Wiederholen Sie Punkt 1 mehrere Male und vergewissern Sie sich dabei, daß die Gewichtung (Größe), Dichte und Platz des Voicings für jeden Akkord ähnlich sind.

3. Notieren Sie Voicings für einen ganzen Chorus und verwenden Sie für jeden Akkord Gruppen von zwei, drei oder vier Voicings aus jeder Kategorie.

4. Notieren Sie Voicings für vier Chorusse. Beginnen Sie im ersten Chorus mit kleineren Voicings, gehen Sie im zweiten Chorus zu größeren, im dritten zu noch größeren und im vierten Chorus zu Oktav-Voicings über.

Sie können jede dieser Übungen zuerst langsam, ohne Aufnahme üben. Ein Metronom oder eine Schlagzeugmaschine kann dabei verwendet werden. Sobald Sie die Voicings in einem ähnlich schnellen Tempo wie die Aufnahme spielen können, versuchen Sie sie mit ihr mitzuspielen.

B. Bei modalen Stücken ist es effektiver, für die Begleitung einfache Vamps - unter Verwendung eines Quarten-Voicings und seines Nachbarn - zu erfinden. Hier sind ein paar Beispiele:

Vous pouvez essayer plusieurs idées pour travailler ces harmonisations:

1. Ecrivez vos harmonisations pour une structure entière, en vous servant d'un accord par mesure. Employez des harmonisations de taille identique et de même densité et jouées dans le même registre du piano.

2. Faite #1 plusieurs fois, en étant sûr que chaque fois la taille, la densité et le placement de ces harmonisations sont identiques.

3. Ecrivez des harmonisations pour une structure entière, en vous servant de groupements de deux, trois ou quatre harmonisations provenant de chaque groupe et pour chaque accord.

4. Ecrivez des harmonisations pour 4 structures. Commencez avec des harmonisations peu fournies, puis plus larges pour la deuxième structure, encore plus larges pour la troisième et des harmonisations "d'octave" pour la quatrième.

Pour chacun de ces exercices, vous désirerez peut être les travailler lentement, sans l'enregistrement. Un métronome ou une boîte à rythmes peuvent être employés pendant votre travail de répétition. Dès que vous arrivez à maîtriser ces accords à un tempo voisin de celui de l'enregistrement, essayez de les jouer avec la piste pré-enregistrée.

B. Une façon efficace d'accompagner dans un morceau modal, est de créer des obstinati simples, en employant des harmonisations en quartes ("quartales") et ses accords voisins. En voici quelques exemples:

C. Here are some ways to create longer phrases, using diatonic voicings from each scale (in each case think *melodically)*:

C. Hier sind einige Möglichkeiten für längere Phrasen, mit diatonischen Voicings aus jeder Skala (in jedem Fall sollten Sie *melodisch* denken):

C. Voici quelques façons de créer des phrases plus longues, en employant des harmonisations diatoniques à partir de chaque gamme (dans chaque cas pensez mélodiquement):

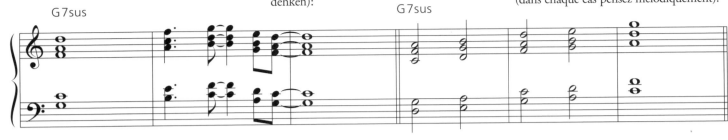

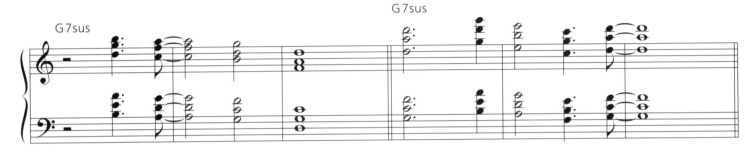

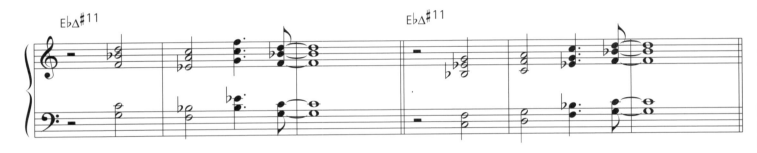

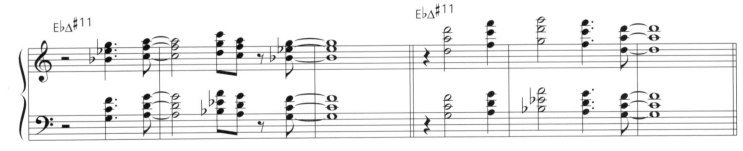

D. Here are some more examples of pan-diatonic comping, in which the right and left hands move in contrary motion:

D. Die folgenden Beispiele zeigen einige Möglichkeiten für pandiatonisches Begleiten, mit der rechten und linken Hand in Gegenbewegung:

D. Voici quelques exemples d'accompagnement supplémentaires "pan-diatoniques" dans lesquels la main gauche et la main droite se déplacent en mouvement contraire:

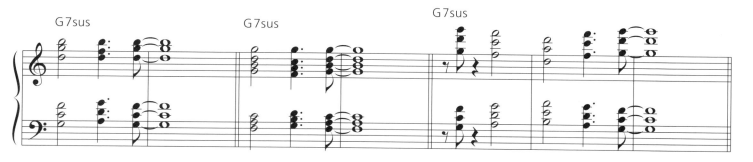

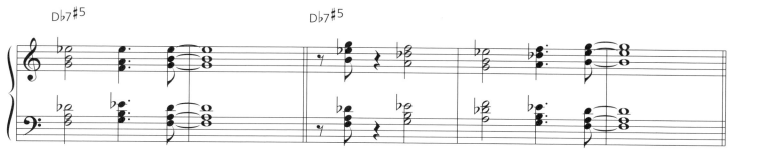

E. Now, start adding some chromatic motion to the comping:

E. Fangen Sie nun an, etwas chromatische Bewegung zur Begleitung dazuzunehmen.

E. Maintenant, commencez à ajouter des mouvements chromatiques à l'accompagnement:

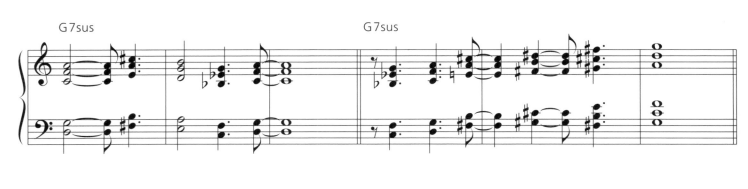

F. It's also possible to chromatically alter each basic chord to create more tension. In this case, you probably wouldn't move the voicings around (as in E).

G7 sus can become:

F. Es ist auch möglich, jeden Grundakkord chromatisch zu alterieren, um mehr Spannung zu erzeugen. In diesem Fall werden Sie wahrscheinlich die Voicings nicht herumbewegen (wie in E).

Aus G7sus kann werden:

F. Il est aussi possible d'altérer chromatiquement chaque accord de base pour créer plus de tension. Dans ce cas, vous ne bougerez probablement pas les harmonisations dans tous les sens (comme dans le paragraphe E).

G7sus peut devenir:

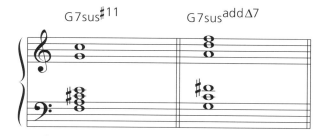

Eᵇ∆ can become:

Aus Eᵇ∆ kann werden:

Eᵇ∆ peut devenir:

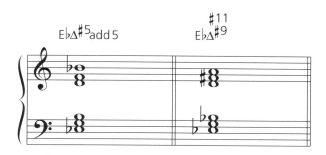

Dᵇ7♯5 can become:

Aus Dᵇ7♯5 kann werden:

Dᵇ7♯5 peut devenir:

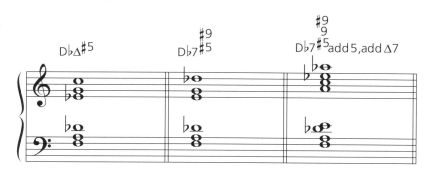

G. You can also try the 'melody' technique (see Karita). One possible melody for the first eight bars would be:

G. Zudem können Sie die 'Melodietechnik' (siehe "Karita") ausprobieren. Eine mögliche Melodie für die ersten acht Takte wäre:

G. Vous pouvez aussi utiliser la technique de la "mélodie" (voir "Karita"). Une mélodie possible pour les premiers huit mesures pourrait être:

Harmonized, it might sound like this:　　　Ausharmonisiert könnte sie so klingen:　　　Harmonisée, elle pourra sonner comme cela:

H. If you are uncomfortable comping at this fast tempo, here are a few exercises you might try:

1. Pick a simple voicng for each chord of the tune. Write each one down, if you'd like. Now, play the piano-less version of "Last Minute", but you don't play any voicings on the piano yet. Just listen to the recording, and feel a half-note pulse (count 1-3-1-3), or even a whole-note pulse (1-1-1-1). Don't try to count every beat. Listen to the whole tune in this manner. Now, start the track over from the beginning. This time, using the voicings you've already picked, try playing these rhythms (at least one chorus for each rhythm):

H. Wenn Sie sich beim Begleiten in diesem schnellen Tempo nicht wohl fühlen, können Sie die folgenden Übungen ausprobieren:

1. Wählen Sie für jeden Akkord ein einfaches Voicing aus. Schreiben Sie jedes auf, falls Sie das möchten. Spielen Sie nun die pianolose Version von "Last Minute", aber spielen Sie noch keine Voicings am Klavier. Hören Sie einfach zu und spüren Sie den Puls in halben Noten (zählen Sie 1-3-1-3) oder in Ganzen (1-1-1-1). Versuchen Sie nicht jeden Schlag zu zählen. Hören Sie sich so das ganze Stück an. Spielen Sie nun die Aufnahme noch einmal. Versuchen Sie diesesmal die Voicings, die Sie bereits ausgewählt haben mit den folgenden Rhythmen zu spielen (wenigstens einen Chorus mit jedem Rhythmus):

H. Si vous n'êtes pas à l'aise pour accompagner à ce tempo très rapide, voici quelque exercices que vous pouvez essayer:

1. Prenez une harmonisation simple pour chaque accord du morceau. Ecrivez-les si vous le désirez. Maintenant, faites jouer la version sans piano de "Last Minute", mais ne jouez pas encore les harmonisations sur le piano. Ecoutez seulement l'enregistrement et ressentez en vous la pulsation en blanche (comptez 1-3-1-3) ou même une pulsation en ronde (1-1-1-1). N'essayez pas de compter tous les temps. Ecoutez le morceau entier de cette manière. Maintenant, recommencez la piste du début. Cette fois, en employant les harmonisations que vous avez déjà choisies, essayez de jouer ces rythmes (ou moins une structure pour chaque rythme):

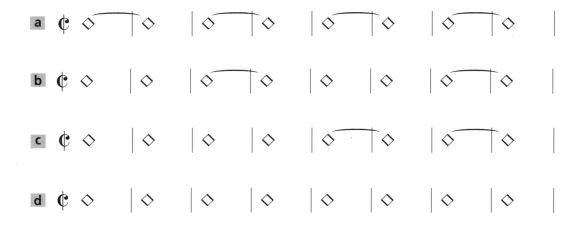

2. Using the same rhythms as in #1, try alternating between a quartal and its neighbor:

2. Verwenden Sie dieselben Rhythmen wie in Punkt 1, versuchen Sie dabei zwischen einem Quarten-Voicing und seinem Nachbarn zu wechseln:

2. En employant les mêmes rythmes que dans #1, essayer d'alterner entre une harmonisation en quartes ("quartale") et les accords voisins.:

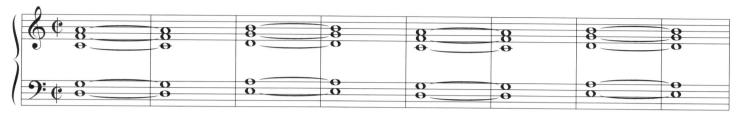

3. Still feeling '1-3-1-3' (or '1-1-1-1'), try these rhythms, using one voicing per chord:

3. Die Zählzeit ist immer noch '1-3-1-3' (oder '1-1-1-1'). Probieren Sie die folgenden Rhythmen mit einem Voicing für jeden Akkord:

3. Tout en continuant à ressentir la pulsation (1-3-1-3) ou (1-1-1-1), essayez ces rythmes en employant une harmonisation par accord:

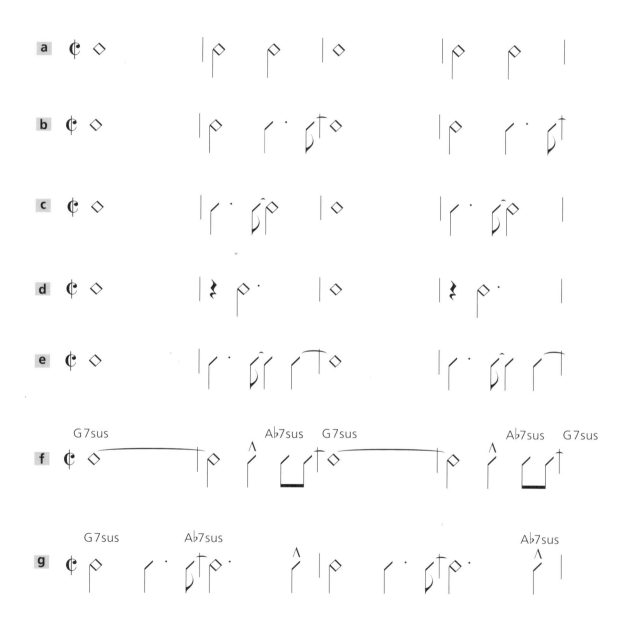

4. Now, using the rhythms from #3, try adding an occasional neighbor voicing:

4. Verwenden Sie als nächstes die Rhythmen von Punkt 3 und versuchen Sie ab und zu Nachbar-Voicings dazuzunehmen.

4. Maintenant, en employant les rythmes du #3, essayez d'ajouter des harmonisations voisines occasionelles:

The important thread that connects all of these exercises is that you are developing the ability to relax and feel a slower half- or whole-note tempo, rather than the quarter-note pulse. As you get stronger with these exercises, you can add more and larger voicings. But keep feeling the slower tempo!

Der rote Faden, der sich durch all diese Übungen zieht, ist der, daß Sie die Fähigkeit entwickeln, ein langsameres Tempo in Halben oder Ganzen zu spüren und nicht den Viertelnotenpuls. Sobald Sie mit diesen Übungen sicherer werden, können Sie mehr und größere Voicings dazunehmen. Aber behalten Sie den Charakter des langsameren Tempos bei!

Le fil important qui relie tous ces exercices, est que vous développiez la capacité de vous détendre et de ressentir un tempo en blanches ou en rondes, plutôt qu'une pulsation en noires. Comme vous devenez plus sûr et plus confiant avec ces exercices, vous pouvez ajouter des harmonisations supplémentaires et plus larges. Mais continuez à percevoir la pulsation à tempo lent.

Suggested Listening

One of the most indispensable sources for learning about comping is recordings of great comping pianists. Here is a list (incomplete I'm sure) of pianists and their recordings which helped this pianist shape his ideas about comping. Most of these recordings are still available, although some have been re-issued under a different title, or as part of a larger anthology.

Earl Hines

"Wheatherbird" (w/Louis Armstrong; the first great duo record)

Teddy Wilson

Recordings w/Billie Holiday, Benny Goodman Trio

Hank Jones

Recordings w/Charlie Parker (e. g. "The Song Is You"); also Thad Jones/Mel Lewis (The Jazz Orchestra)

Bud Powell

"Massey Hall Concert" (w/Dizzy Gillespie, Charlie Parker, et al)

Red Garland

Recordings w/Miles Davis (for Prestige and Columbia labels), John Coltrane (Prestige)

Horace Silver

His own small group recordings on Blue Note; also early Jazz Messengers recordings (w/Art Blakey, Clifford Brown, et al)

Ritchie Powell

Recordings w/Clifford Brown/Max Roach

Bill Evans

Recordings w/Miles Davis (especially "Kind Of Blue", Columbia), his own trio recordings (for comping for bass solos)

Wynton Kelly

w/Miles Davis Quintet
"Live at the Blackhawk", "Friday Night", "Live at the Blackhawk", "Saturday Night" (one of the textbooks on small group comping!); also recordings w/Wes Montgomery, Cannonball Adderley, many others

Herbie Hancock

w/Miles Davis (especially "Four And More", "My Funny Valentine", and "E. S. P."); also many recordings as leader and sideman for Blue Note (especially "Maiden Voyage")

Hörempfehlungen

Eine der unentbehrlichsten Quellen, um über das Begleiten zu lernen, sind Aufnahmen der großen 'Begleitpianisten'. Hier ist eine Liste (ich bin sicher, sie ist nicht vollständig) von Pianisten und ihren Aufnahmen, die dem Autor geholfen haben, seine Ideen über das Begleiten zu formen. Die meisten dieser Aufnahmen sind immer noch erhältlich, obwohl manche unter einem anderen Titel oder als Teil einer umfangreicheren Anthologie, wiederveröffentlicht wurden.

Earl Hines

"Wheatherbird" (mit Louis Armstrong; die erste großartige Duoplatte)

Teddy Wilson

Aufnahmen mit Billie Holiday und dem Benny Goodman Trio

Hank Jones

Aufnahmen mit Charlie Parker (z.B. "The Song Is You"); und Thad Jones/Mel Lewis (The Jazz Orchestra)

Bud Powell

"Massey Hall Concert" (mit Dizzy Gillespie, Charlie Parker)

Red Garland

Aufnahmen mit Miles Davis (für die Label Prestige und Columbia), John Coltrane (Prestige)

Horace Silver

Seine eigenen Aufnahmen mit kleinen Gruppen für Blue Note; außerdem frühe Jazz Messengers Aufnahmen (mit Art Blakey, Clifford Brown)

Ritchie Powell

Aufnahmen mit Clifford Brown/Max Roach

Bill Evans

Aufnahmen mit Miles Davis (insbesondere "Kind Of Blue", Columbia), seine eigenen Trioaufnahmen (Begleitung der Baßsoli)

Wynton Kelly

mit dem Miles Davis Quintet
"Live at the Blackhawk", "Friday Night", "Live at the Blackhawk", "Saturday Night" (eine Enzyklopädie für das Begleiten in einer Combo); außerdem Aufnahmen mit Wes Montgomery, Cannonball Adderley und vielen anderen

Suggestions pour l'écoute

Une des plus indispensables sources pour étudier l'accompagnement est l'écoute des enregistrements des pianistes qui sont de grands accompagnateurs. Voici une liste (incomplète, j'en suis sûr) des pianistes et de leurs enregistrements qui aidera le pianiste que vous êtes, à façonner ses idées par rapport à l'accompagnement. La plupart de ces enregistrements sont toujours disponibles, même si certains ont été ré-édités sous un titre différent, ou comme partie d'une plus grande anthologie.

Earl Hines

"Wheatherbird" (avec Louis Armstrong; le premier grand enregistrement en duo)

Teddy Wilson

Enregistrements avec Billie Holiday, Benny Goodman trio

Hank Jones

Enregistrements avec Charlie Parker ("The Song Is You"); aussi avec Thad Jones/Mel Lewis (The Jazz Orchestra)

Bud Powell

"Massey Hall Concert" (avec Dizzy Gillespie, Charlie Parker, etc ...)

Red Garland

Enregistrements avec Miles Davis (pour les labels Prestige et Columbia), John Coltrane (Prestige).

Horace Silver

Enregistrements avec ses propres petits groupes sur Blue Note et aussi les premiers enregistrements avec les Jazz Messengers recordings (avec Art Blakey, Clifford Brown, etc ...)

Ritchie Powell

Enregistrements avec Clifford Brown/Max Roach

Bill Evans

Enregistrements avec Miles Davis (particulièrement "Kind Of Blue", Columbia). Les enregistrements avec son propre trio (pour l'accompagnement des solos de basse).

Wynton Kelly

Enregistrements avec Miles Davis Quintet "Live at the Blackhawk", "Friday Night", et "Live at the Blackhawk", "Saturday Night" (l'un, des meilleurs manuels sur l'accompagnement en petite formation!); et aussi les enregistrements avec Wes Montgomery, Cannonball Adderley, et beaucoup d'autres

Thelonious Monk

Quartet recordings for Columbia (Warning: Do Not Try This At Home! (smile)

Cedar Walton

Recordings w/Art Blakey & the Jazz Messengers (especially "Free for All"); also his own small group recordings

Jaki Byard

Recordings w/Charles Mingus; also his own small group recordings for Prestige; also recordings w/Eric Dolphy

McCoy Tyner

Recordings w/John Coltrane (especially "A Love Supreme" and "Ballads"); also many Blue Note recordings as leader (e. g. "The Real McCoy") and as sideman (e. g. Joe Henderson, "In 'n Out")

Ronnie Matthews

Freddie Hubbard, "Breaking Point" (Blue Note); also recorded w/Johnny Griffin

Chick Corea

His own "Tones for Joan's Bones"; also recordings w/Miles Davis, and Stan Getz (especially "Sweet Rain")

Roland Hanna

Recordings w/Thad Jones/Mel Lewis

Keith Jarrett

Quartet recordings w/Jan Garbarek, Dewey Redman

Kenny Barron

Recordings w/Freddie Hubbard, Stan Getz

Hal Galper

Recordings w/Phil Woods Quartet/Quintet; also, his own "Reach Out"

Richie Beirach

Recordings w/David Liebman and John Abercrombie (Many duo recordings; also two different Liebman quartets: "Lookout Farm", and "Quest")

Herbie Hancock

mit Miles Davis (insbesondere "Four And More", "My Funny Valentine" und "E. S. P."); außerdem viele Aufnahmen als Leader und Sideman für Blue Note (insbesondere "Maiden Voyage")

Thelonious Monk

Quartettaufnahmen für Columbia (Warnung: Probieren Sie das nicht zu Hause! (lacht)

Cedar Walton

Aufnahmen mit Art Blakey & the Jazz Messengers (insbesondere "Free for All"); außerdem Aufnahmen mit seinen eigenen Combos

Jaki Byard

Aufnahmen mit Charles Mingus; außerdem seine Aufnahmen mit eigenen Combos für Prestige und Aufnahmen mit Eric Dolphy

McCoy Tyner

Aufnahmen mit John Coltrane (insbesondere "A Love Supreme" und "Ballads") ; außerdem viele Blue Note Aufnahmen als Leader (z.B. "The Real McCoy") und als Sideman (Joe Henderson, "In 'n Out")

Ronnie Matthews

Freddie Hubbard, "Breaking Point" (Blue Note) ; zudem Aufnahmen mit Johnny Griffin

Chick Corea

Unter eigenem Namen "Tones for Joan's Bones"; außerdem Aufnahmen mit Miles Davis und Stan Getz (insbesondere "Sweet Rain")

Roland Hanna

Aufnahmen mit Thad Jones/Mel Lewis

Keith Jarrett

Quartettaufnahmen mit Jan Garbarek und Dewey Redman

Kenny Barron

Aufnahmen mit Freddie Hubbard, Stan Getz

Hal Galper

Aufnahmen mit dem Phil Woods Quartet/ Quintet ; außerdem, unter seinem Namen "Reach Out"

Richie Beirach

Aufnahmen mit David Liebman und John Abercrombie (viele Duoaufnahmen und zwei verschiedene Liebman-Quartette: "Lookout Farm" und "Quest")

Herbie Hancock

Enregistrements avec Miles Davis (particulièrement "Four And More", "My Funny Valentine", and "E. S. P."); et aussi de nombreux enregistrements comme chef d'orchestre et musicien pour Blue Note (particulièrement "Maiden Voyage")

Thelonious Monk

Les enregistrements en quartet pour Columbia (Attention: N'essayez pas ceci à la maison! (il sourit)

Cedar Walton

Enregistrements avec Art Blakey & the Jazz Messengers (particulièrement "Free for All"); et aussi ses enregistrements en petite formation

Jaki Byard

Les enregistrements avec Charles Mingus; et aussi ses enregistrements en petit formation pour Prestige et aussi les enregistrements pour Eric Dolphy

McCoy Tyner

Les enregistrements avec John Coltrane (particulièrement "A Love Supreme" et "Ballads") ; aussi plusieurs enregistrements pour Blue Note comme chef d'orchestre ("The Real McCoy") et comme musicien (Joe Henderson, "In 'n Out")

Ronnie Matthews

Freddie Hubbard, "Breaking Point" (Blue Note); et aussi avec Johnny Griffin

Chick Corea

Son enregistrement "Tones for Joan's Bones"; et aussi les enregistrements avec Miles Davis, et Stan Getz (particulièrement "Sweet Rain")

Roland Hanna

Enregistrements avec Thad Jones/Mel Lewis

Keith Jarrett

Enregistrements en quartet avec Jan Garbarek et Dewey Redman

Kenny Barron

Enregistrements avec Freddie Hubbard, Stan Getz

Hal Galper

Enregistrements avec Phil Woods Quartet/ Quintet; et aussi son disque "Reach Out"

Richie Beirach

Enregistrements avec David Liebman and John Abercrombie (beaucoup d' enregistrements en duo; et aussi deux quartets de Liebman: "Lookout Farm" et "Quest")

Many of these players are still active. Check them out when you can, on recordings or, better yet, live (most of them are nice human beings and surprisingly approachable and willing to answer questions!). Also check out other players not on the above list, such as Jo Anne Brackeen, Mulgrew Miller, James Williams, Kenny Kirkland, Geoff Keezer, Benny Green, Renee Rosnes, George Cables, Kirk Lightsey, and Marcus Roberts.

One final observation: to learn to do anything well you must study it, and practice it, but most importantly, you have to Do It! And when you think that you've done it enough, Do It Some More! Then, when it really feels like you've got it together, Do It Some More! Then Do It Again tomorrow, and tomorrow, and tomorrow, and tomorrow......

Viele dieser Pianisten sind immer noch aktiv. Hören Sie sie sich ihre Aufnahmen an, wann immer sie können, oder noch besser, gehen Sie zu ihren Auftritten, solange es noch möglich ist (die meisten sind nette Menschen und überraschenderweise ansprechbar und willig, Fragen zu beantworten!). Hören Sie sich auch Pianisten an, die nicht in der obigen Liste enthalten sind, z. B. Jo Anne Brackeen, Mulgrew Miller, James Williams, Kenny Kirkland, Geoff Keezer, Benny Green, Renee Rosnes, George Cables, Kirk Lightsey und Marcus Roberts.

Eine letzte Bemerkung: Um etwas zu können, müssen Sie es lernen und üben, aber noch wichtiger, sie müssen es tun! Und wenn Sie glauben, Sie haben es genug getan, tun Sie es noch mehr! Dann, wenn Sie wirklich das Gefühl haben, Sie können es, tun Sie es noch mehr! Morgen, und Übermorgen und.......

Beaucoup de ces musiciens sont encore en activité. Ecoutez-les pour vérifier ces suggestions, sur des enregistrements ou, mieux encore, en direct (la plupart d°entre eux sont des êtres humains aimables, étonnamment accessible et voulant répondre aux questions!). Ecoutez aussi d'autres musiciens qui ne sont pas sur cette liste, tels que Jo Anne Brackeen, Mulgrew Miller, James Williams, Kenny Kirkland, Geoff Keezer, Benny Green, Renee Rosnes, George Cables, Kirk Lightsey et Marcus Roberts.

Une observation finale: pour apprendre à faire quelquechose correctement, vous devez étudier et travailler, répéter cette "chose", mais ce qui est plus important encore vous devez le faire, le jouer! Et grand vous pensez que vous l'avez assez fait, faites le encore un peu plus! Puis quand vous sentez vraiment que vous avez réussi à mettre tout cela ensemble, faites le encore un peu plus! Puis faites le encore demain, et demain, et demain, et demain.......

About the author

Jim McNeely was born in Chicago. He received his degree in composition from the University of Illinois in 1975, at which time he moved to New York City. Since then he has become part of the international jazz scene.

Jim received his first critical acclaim as pianist with the groups of trumpeters Ted Curson and Chet Baker. In 1978 he joined the Thad Jones/Mel Lewis Jazz Orchestra. He spent six years as a featured soloist with that band and its successor, Mel Lewis and the Jazz Orchestra. Meanwhile, 1981 saw the beginning of Jim's 4-year tenure as pianist/composer with the Stan Getz Quartet. Since 1990 he has held the piano chair in the Phil Woods Quintet. At the same time he leads his own trio, freelances with greats such as Joe Henderson and David Liebman, and appears as soloist at concerts and festivals in places varied as Finland, Australia, and Cleveland.

Jim has appeared as a sideman on recordings with Mel Lewis's band, Stan Getz, David Liebman, Phil Woods, and many others. He currently has six albums of his own to his credit. His reputation as an original composer/arranger for large jazz band continues to grow as well. His most recent recorded work includes projects with the Stockholm Jazz Orchestra and the West German radio (W.D.R.) Big Band

Teaching is also an important element of Jim's work. Since 1981 he has been part of the jazz faculty at New York University, where he is Adjunct Resident Artist in Jazz Studies. In addition he teaches at William Patterson College in Wayne, N.J. He is also co-director of the B.M.I. Jazz Composer's Workshop.

Über den Autor

Jim McNeely wurde in Chicago geboren. 1975 absolvierte er die Universität von Illinois im Fach Komposition und zog nach New York. Seither gehört er zur internationalen Jazzszene.

Erste kritische Beachtung fand er als Pianist mit den Gruppen der Trompeter Ted Curson und Chet Baker. 1978 trat er in das *Thad Jones/Mel Lewis Jazz Orchestra* ein. Sechs Jahre war er einer der Hauptsolisten dieser Band und der des Nachfolgers, Mel Lewis. 1981 begann eine 4jährige Zusammenarbeit als Pianist und Komponist mit dem *Stan Getz Quartet*. Seit 1990 ist er Pianist im *Phil Woods Quintet*. Gleichzeitig leitet er sein eigenes Trio, spielt mit großen Musikern wie Joe Henderson und David Liebman. Zudem tritt er als Gastsolist bei Festivals an den verschiedensten Plätzen wie Finnland, Australien oder Cleveland auf.

Jim wirkte bei Aufnahmen mit Mel Lewis' Band, Stan Getz, David Liebman, Phil Woods und vielen anderen als Sideman mit. Er hat bisher sechs Platten unter seinem eigenen Namen veröffentlicht. Sein Ruf als eigenständiger Komponist und Arrangeur für Jazzorchester steigt ständig. Seine aktuellsten Arbeiten schließen Projekte für das *Stockholm Jazz Orchestra*, und für die WDR Big Band, Köln mit ein.

Unterrichten ist ein wichtiges Element in seiner Arbeit. Seit 1981 gehört er zur Jazzfakultät der *New York University*, wo er zur Zeit als *Adjunct Resident Artist in Jazz Studies* tätig ist. Zusätzlich unterrichtet er am *William Patterson College* in Wayne, New Jersey. Zudem ist er Codirektor des *B.M.I. Jazz Composer's Workshop*.

A propos de l'auteur

Jim McNeely naquit à Chicago. Il reçut son diplôme en composition de l'Université de l'Illinois en 1975, et c'est à cette époque qu'il s'établit à New York. C'est à partir de cette époque qu'il devint une partie de la scène internationale du jazz.

Jim reçut ses premières acclamations, de la part des critiques, en tant que pianiste, dans les groupes des trompettistes Ted Curson et Chet Baker. En 1978 il se joignit au *Thad Jones/Mel Lewis Jazz Orchestra*. Il passa, en tant que soliste, six années dans cet orchestre ainsi que dans l'orchestre qui lui succéda, le *Mel Lewis and the Jazz Orchestra*. En même temps, 1981 vit le début des quatre années que Jim passa au poste de pianiste/compositeur dans le quartet de Stan Getz. Depuis 1990, il occupe la chaise du piano dans le quintet de Phil Woods. Dans le même temps, il dirige son propre trio, en travaillant en *Free Lance* avec des célébrités telles que Joe Henderson et David Liebman, se produisant comme soliste dans des concerts et des festivals dans des endroits aussi variés que la Finlande, l'Australie, ou Cleveland.

Jim apparaît en tant que musicien sur des enregistrements avec l'orchestre de Mel Lewis, Stan Getz, David Liebman, Phil Woods et bien d'autres encore. Il possède actuellement six albums sous son nom à son actif. La réputation en temps que compositeur et arrangeur original pour grand orchestre de jazz continue à se développer. Les plus récentes oeuvres enregistrées incluent des projets avec le *Stockholm Jazz Orchestra* et le *Grand Orchestre De La Radio Allemande De L'Ouest (W.D.R.)*.

L'enseignement est aussi un élément important du travail de Jim. Depuis 1981 il a été un membre de la *Faculté de Jazz de L'Université De New York* où il est actuellement un *Artiste Residant Adjoint Pour Les Études De Jazz*. De plus il enseigne au *William Patterson College*, dans le Wayne, New Jersey. Il est aussi co-directeur du *BMI Jazz Composer's Workshop*.